THIS BOOK BELONGS TO

FROM

DATE

"For I know the plans I have for you," declares the LORD, *"plans to prosper and not to harm you, plans to give you hope and a future." Jeremiah 29:11*

HINDSIGHT

advice from those who have been there

CONCORDIA PUBLISHING HOUSE • SAINT LOUIS

OUR THANKS TO OUR YOUNG ADULT AUTHORS

Bethany Albers
Roy Askins
Ellie Bach
Marcus Baikie
Timothy Bayer
Heather Croucher
Katie Dargatz
Joshua Dehne
Ross Engel
Cadet John Ethredge
Nate Farber
Matthew T. Frick
Macie Smith
Todd Leifer
Susan Leistico
Matt Makela
Katie Maske
Elizabeth Meckler
Johanna Mumme
Jonathan Mumme
Christine Oberdeck
Jessica Paul
Kristen Reeb
Julianna Shults
Anna Shadday
Brianne Victor
Lisa Widlowski
Amanda Wilhelm
Amber Morris
Josh Moldenhauer

Library of Congress Cataloging-in-Publication Data

Hindsight: advice from those who have been there.

     p. cm.

   ISBN 0-7586-0378-9

  1. High school graduates—Religious life. 2. Young adults—Religious
life. 3. High school graduates—Prayer books and devotions—English.
4. Young adults—Prayer books and devotions—English. I. Concordia
Publishing House.

   BV4529.2.H56 2005

   248.8′3—dc22

                        2004023367

1 2 3 4 5 6 7 8 9 10   14 13 12 11 10 09 08 07 06 05

INTRODUCTION

Have you ever noticed that things in life seem a lot clearer when you view them as part of your past? Growing up involves making choices that sometimes seem a little scary. Sadly the choices don't get easier the older you get. It's enough to make you want to go back to being a little kid sometimes.

The good news is that our Lord understands the challenge of making wise choices. In His Word God promises to guide us in the choices we make. He tells us that His love and forgiveness are there, even when we mess up or make the wrong choice.

In this book you will read the stories written by young people like yourself. They are in college, the armed services, or the work force. The authors of these reflections have the blessing of being able to look back at the choices they've made and how God was with them. As you read their stories, may you be blessed in your journey of faith.

RECOGNITION

Be made new in the attitude of your minds;
and put on the new self, created to be like God
in true righteousness and holiness. Ephesians 4:23–24

WORKING FOR WHAT?

Read: Luke 12:13–34

"What do you want to be when you grow up?" Surely someone has asked you this before. Time and time again, family members and others hound you with this question. People start asking when you're in kindergarten and they don't stop until you graduate! Even after graduation day, their question still lingers in conversations.

Do you have an answer to this common question? You might have high expectations, wanting to go to law school, become a psychiatrist, or study engineering. Maybe you're still undecided—that is not a bad thing. Frequently, we respond to the question by saying, "I'm not sure yet." Some even add the phrase, "Whatever makes a lot of money!"

While sometimes this response is merely a joke to release the tension of the question, sometimes it is an honest response. If an honest response, this is a warning sign for unhappiness. Oh sure, money will bring some happiness, like the ability to buy what you want or the peace of security. But is this true joy?

If you know what you want to do for a career, does it use your God-given gifts to better serve the world? All too often, salary is the first thing people look at when deciding on an occupation. While money seems to be the only thing that can bring true happiness, the illusion is that it will save them from their fears.

Oftentimes we use money as a way to say to God "I can do it." We see ourselves as capable of caring for ourselves—

independent of God. Money sets us apart from the rest of society as we fall into the trap that we are better, saved by our financial abilities, good character, or charity.

Now, money in itself is not a bad thing. People need money to provide for themselves and others. Even prosperity is a blessing—God blessed the man in the parable with material wealth. But the man's attitude toward his prosperity was sinful. He did not use his gifts to serve others. And in his greed, the man forgot about God—the One who gave him this gift!

This parable has an obvious lesson: while worldly riches are temporary, being rich in God will make you rich forever. Unlike money, God's riches never fail. You may have all of the diamonds, cars, or clothes in the world; but without God, you will never know true happiness. Diamonds can be lost. Cars can break down. Clothes can tear. But God will always be there for you. He sent his Son, Jesus Christ, to die for your sins so you can live forever in heaven—a place so full of riches that it puts all earthly possessions to shame. Take your trust out of worldly wealth and invest your trust in Christ. Realize He is always with you and He will never fail you.

> Heavenly Father, the world can be so confusing. I am led to believe that only money brings happiness, but You have shown me that this is not true. You are the only path to true happiness. Help me to realize that with You I have nothing else to fear. Amen.

LABELED

Read: Galatians 3:26–28

Labels are inescapable in high school, and, I hate to break it to you, they're inescapable outside of school too: college, work, whatever. There are jocks, nerds, blacks, whites, guys, girls, rich, poor, good-looking, and ugly; and that's just a handful. And, of course, with labels comes status. You know that there is a hierarchy in the world based on your label. It's just the way it is. Some groups are better than others and it's been like that since the earliest days of creation.

While a "pecking order" may be true in the world, it certainly has no place in the Church. As St. Paul writes, everyone who is baptized has "put on Christ." Therefore, to God, the old labels are not there. There is no race, no gender, no socio-economic status, no political affiliation, no disparity in talents, because none of those things can affect salvation. There is only Christ and His righteousness, freely given to all believers.

While God wants everyone to be faithful from the beginning of our lives, those who come to faith later in life are saved. What's most important to God is that we do come to faith. In the parable of the laborers (Matthew 20:1–16), Jesus speaks of a generous master who paid the laborers who worked one hour the same wage as the laborers who worked all day. While this seems unfair in our world of time clocks and contracts, in that time laborers would be unemployed if it weren't for the master finding them and hiring them. God doesn't work on time clocks. God gives the same gift of eternal life to those baptized as infants and lifelong Christians as He does to the horrible lifelong sinner who repents and believes on his deathbed. It may not seem fair, but if things were fair, we'd be condemned to hell and Jesus Christ wouldn't have had to die.

But Christ did die. He did the unfair thing to Himself and was crucified for our sins, "and not only for ours, but also for the sins of the whole world" (1 John 2:2). Regardless who they are in an earthly sense, God "wants all men to be saved and to come to a knowledge of the truth" (1 Timothy 2:4). Even the early Church struggled with this notion. St. Peter himself, one of Jesus' most trusted apostles, needed a vision from God to see that the Gentiles needed the Gospel just as much as the Jews did (Acts 10:9–16).

On earth, labels matter. That's not fair sometimes. But to God, only one label matters: the holy blood of Jesus Christ. That wasn't fair to Him, either, and we praise Him for it.

Lord Jesus Christ, who came to earth to do the unfair thing and die for our sins, we pray that the Holy Spirit would make us one in You, to see past the labels we place on one another, and give all glory to You, through whom we pray. Amen.

TESTIMONY? WHAT TESTIMONY?

Read: Revelation 3:14–16

Testimony. It was my first assignment of my composition class my freshman year of college and I was intimidated. Write about your faith? What is that for an assignment? I was intimidated not only to share my faith with others but also how to share it. It seemed like all of the other girls on my floor had "testimony," some life altering event or another that spurred their faith to grow. It seemed like I was the abnormal one who just paddled through the day. My faith was there. I went to church and I confessed it. It was there, but I just didn't know how to share it.

I was intimidated because the assignment asked me to look at my own faith and assess it. It numbly chipped away at my brain asking for the thoughts I had starved from that area of my life for so long. My faith was there as I made decisions. Often it felt like the angel-devil cartoons as I wrestled with issues and decisions. I felt my faith as my friends made decisions about drugs, sex, alcohol, parties. I knew the right and the wrong and wrestled to put all of it behind me. I figured that would make some sort of a testimony. But still I struggled with the basic question, "What is faith?"

Faith. In high school I once heard a friend use the term "on-fire-for-God Christian." In my conservative background we did not use such phrases. She explained the term by explaining Revelation 3:14–16 and the term "lukewarm." Many of you may know this term. Neither hot nor cold. Lukewarm is in the middle. John writes seven letters to seven churches in Revelation. This one, written to Laodicea, scorns them for being lukewarm. They were on-the-fence Christians, neither hating and denying God nor praising Him. They were the quiet ones listening and trying to change the topic. Convinced of His presence but unwilling to admit it.

As I juggled the assigned task and my swirling thoughts, the paper emerged with a testimony woven into it. No it was not an experience or event, it was my sin in the spotlight of the Law and overwhelmed with the sunlight of the Gospel. My testimony of faith was *mine*. It was one of juggling my faith and life, so the latter would reflect the former and not the reverse. For years I was a fence dweller, trying to hide up there yet seen by both sides for the fake I am. The Lord who is the Lord of all seven churches loved all of them, died for all of them. Where some are strong, I was weak, but the Lord loves me still. Where I was on the fence, convicted in the spotlight of indecision, Christ was on the cross dying for that sin. The testimony is *not mine*, but *His*. It is His love, and His death, His decision to save me.

> Dear Lord, at times I sit on the fence, denying You, ignoring my faith. I am sorry that I have sinned against You. Thank You for loving me so much that you sent Your Son to die on the cross for my sin. Thank You for promising to love me always even when I am faltering. Let Your Word grow in my heart, strengthen my faith in You. Amen.

PURPOSE

Read: Psalm 103 and 2 Corinthians 5:11–21

You read a lot about purpose these days. It's in books ranging from *The Purpose-Driven Life* to *40 Days of Purpose.* For hundreds of years people have struggled with finding their individual purpose in life. As a young adult it will be one of the utmost challenges you face. You'll be forced, by yourself or others, to look at why you do the things you do, the purpose of your earthly existence. Resolving those issues, at least to some degree, will help provide you with direction and encouragement in the years and decades to come.

Being a Christian, someone really connected to the saving power of Jesus Christ, is something that impacts every area and aspect of your life. This of course includes your purpose. The words of 2 Corinthians 5 provide both the why and how of our life's purpose. Why do we do the things we do? Why act as bearers of light and purity in a dark world? Because "Christ's love compels us." The love of Christ is so deep and consuming that it covers all of our sins and faults and weaknesses and failures. And as a result, we can't help but want to share that love with others, whether witnessing directly to them with our words or indirectly through our actions.

That leads us to the how, which is living for others and not ourselves. In the world you'll find no shortage of people who live with a selfish, "I'm only going to look out for myself" attitude. Left to ourselves, we would be just like that. But Christ's love in us changes that, and He calls us to a life of love and service toward others. How that plays out in our lives is different for each of us because we all have different vocations, but the overall purpose is the same for all.

We don't serve others simply for the benefit of unbelievers (i.e., evangelism) but for our brothers and sisters in Christ as well. Remember that one of the reasons Christ placed His followers into one large body called the Church is so we might "spur one another on toward love and good deeds" (Hebrews 10:24). What's so amazing and comforting on top of all this is that God provides us with the Holy Spirit who gives us the power to do all this and more in His name. God provides the goal, the motivation, and the means.

> Dear Lord, thank You for the mercy and grace You've so richly showered upon me. Help me in greater ways to share that love with others. Thank You for allowing me to live in a world so full of opportunities to serve You. Thank You for providing, in Christ, a purpose for living. Please give me the power to remember Your purpose for my life and to serve You with an undivided heart. In Jesus' name I pray. Amen.

WHO AM I?

Read: Psalm 139:13–18 and 1 John 3:1–2

In high school I constantly questioned my identity. I knew there was more to me than my friends, teachers, and family could see, but I wasn't sure what that was. I wasn't entirely sure what I thought college would answer, but I hoped it would help. When I arrived, I found I was just a number, one of thousands of new students. I was defined by my class year, my major, my financial aid package, my student ID number, and my Social Security number. I had yet to answer the question: Who am I?

In searching for a solution, I listened to all the wrong voices. I listened to voices from friends, family, society, and university, as well as the voices within myself. Each one was trying to define me. In listening to the competing voices, I lost sight of the truth. My sins of doubt and the temptation to trust those voices separated me from God. I lost my true identity.

Jesus did not lose His identity to those questioning voices. At twelve, Jesus knew who He was and what He was to do. Wouldn't it be nice to know your identity at twelve? The reassuring answer is we do! Jesus did face voices, though not the inner voices that questioned His identity. He faced the voice of the world that refused to accept His identity, family and friends who could not see Him as Savior, accusations from the Pharisees and the Sadducees who said He was acting under Satan's authority. Even Christ's beloved disciples, try as they might, could not understand who He was. The angels named Him, Satan recognized Him, and demons knew Him, but many did not understand who He truly was until His death and resurrection. In that action, Jesus made it known that He was the Savior, the Son of God. In Christ's sacrifice, our sins of doubt are forgiven. We are tied to Christ's death and resurrection through our Baptism. In Him, we find who we truly are: the sons and daughters of the Father. In His great love for us, the Father gave the Son so we may know our true identity as children of God.

Somewhere along the road all of this finally clicked for me. Even if at times I don't really know myself, there's someone who knows me more intimately than I can imagine. He formed me with the same hands that formed the world, He redeemed me with His blood because He loves me so much, and He made me His child so I would know my identity in Him.

Sometimes we're unsure of ourselves, sometimes we don't know who we are, but we know to Whom we belong. One thing is always true: despite our own doubts, God loves us. His love and forgiveness are shown forth through the Sacraments; in them we are reassured of our identity as His children. And it just gets better from here (1 John 3:2).

> Father, thank You for making us Your children. Let us never lose sight of our true identity, reminding us through Your Word, our Baptism, and the Sacraments. In Jesus' name we pray. Amen.

RECONSIDERATION

In this you greatly rejoice, though now for a little while you may have had to suffer grief in all kinds of trials. These have come so that your faith—of greater worth than gold, which perishes even though refined by fire— may be proved genuine and may result in praise, glory, and honor when Jesus Christ is revealed. 1 Peter 1:6–7

SON NOT A SERVANT

Read: Luke 15:17–20

As a recent graduate, the world is your oyster. Parties, ceremonies, gifts, recognition—it's one of the best times of your life. People are all too ready to shake your hand and give you a word of congratulations. But they don't tell you the downside, do they? This is only going to last for a few weeks. After this could be college (welcome to life as a lowly freshman again) or a job (snot-nosed rookie) or life on your own (rent's due again?!). Guess what—you're back at square one—from king of the hill to just another needle in the haystack. Of course, you don't expect to stay there. There are a lot of good things awaiting you in your future: College graduation, post-graduate degrees, promotions at work, marriage, family, retirement—but that all seems so far off.

The prodigal son had just crashed after his peak, too. Living the highlife had led to this: sitting in a pigsty eating slop (literally). One would expect your post-graduation experience to be better. Nevertheless, he knew he had a place to go, and the only way he knew he was going to get there was by himself. It was too late to be an honored son; servitude was his only hope.

His father had other plans, though. While the son was "a long way off," still trudging his way back home, his father saw him and ran to him, completely obliterating any plans the son had of returning as a servant. His father gave him something better than he ever expected.

Too often, when we hit rock bottom, we think we have our escape all planned out. We decide that we have a place to go and the only way we're getting there is by pulling ourselves up by our bootstraps. This is not so. Our heavenly Father isn't content in letting us do the dirty work ourselves. His plan and blessings for us are head and shoulders above anything we can conceive. Nowhere is this more evident than at the cross. Just as the father humiliated himself by running in the dusty countryside to his son, so also did the Son, Jesus Christ, humble Himself by coming to earth in human flesh to die for us (Philippians 2:8). Through His death and resurrection, He broke our servitude to sin and gave us status as children of God.

From the bottom, it looks like the top is a long way off. Sometimes it actually is. Regardless, we have a sure promise of Christ that He will not leave us to ourselves, but He will be with us always, throughout good times and bad, to the end of eternal life, which is exactly "what God has prepared for those who love Him" (1 Corinthians 2:9).

Heavenly Father, who loves us and gives us more than we deserve or can imagine, grant that everything we do might be guided by Your hand, knowing that You are with us always. Through Jesus Christ, our Lord. Amen.

DOUBTS

Read: 1 Peter 1:8

"Is there really a God? Do I really have faith in Him or do I just believe because my parents do? If I were to die, am I absolutely certain I would go to heaven? Do heaven and hell really exist? Did someone just make up all this stuff? Do I really need a Savior? Does God really love me or do people just say that?" These heavy questions were the doubts that I found swimming through my head and eating away at me during my first two years at college. I had met so many new people, some like me and some completely different on all sorts of levels. I have always been a Christian. My dad is a pastor, my mom a Christian school teacher. I have gone to Christian schools my entire life. Being outside of my box in college, I found myself dealing with all sorts of questions that caused me to doubt my faith. I met teachers who promoted issues my faith did not agree with and students' whose lifestyles contradicted mine. I often wished I could go back to being three or four years old and have that child-like faith that believed without any questions.

New people, college, a phase in life, a crisis—whatever you want to call all of my doubts, I came through it. I came to basically the same conclusions.

First, my Baptism made me a child of God and granted me faith. Through those Baptism waters and God's Word faith was planted in me. 1 Peter 3:21 says, "And this water symbolizes Baptism that now saves you." My salvation is secure with God.

Second, the devil is a liar. Jesus says in John 8:44, "for

he [the devil] is a liar and the father of lies." The devil enjoys telling us "There is no God," "You don't need a Savior," and numerous other lies. Those doubts may be the devil trying to pull you away from the truth.

Third, God tells us that through faith in His Son's death and resurrection we receive eternal life in heaven as a free gift. How do we know this is the truth? Hebrews 11:1 says, "Faith is being sure of what we hope for and certain of what we do not see." That sums everything up. We can't see that God is there, but by faith we know He is. Although we might ask, "How do I know I have faith?" our faith is not dependent on us. Only God can grant faith; it is a gift from Him. Ephesians 2:8, "For it is by grace you have been saved through faith—and this is not from yourselves it is the gift of God." Therefore, rejoice! God's plan for salvation and His Word are true!

When those doubts begin to swim through your head, remember that God promises in Joshua 1:5, "I will never leave you nor forsake you." No matter how many questions I asked, God continued to be with me and He will stay with you as well.

> Dear Lord, Sometimes it is hard to believe that You are there. Grant me faith to be confident in Your promises. Thank You for never leaving me and providing me with the truth in the Bible. Help me to turn to Your Word in times of doubt. Lord, help me to "live by faith, not by sight." In Your precious name. Amen.

IT DOESN'T MAKE SENSE

Read: Isaiah 55:8–9

"Another final paper at the end of the semester. That will make three 10–15 page papers in less than three weeks. Two of them require research." I dropped my backpack on the floor and looked at my roommate in disgust. "This doesn't make sense."

I never understood why professors like to assign the longest papers at the end of the term when they all knew you were overworked finishing projects and studying for finals. It never has made sense to me. Sure I could logically conceive that the professors were all trying to cram the last of the chapters or units into us, one last book or grain of knowledge, or even that they were trying to come up with some last assignment to assess our knowledge, but I still firmly believed that they should plan it together. It did not make sense.

A lot of things in life I found to be like that. Friends I met had experienced things so awful that it seemed surreal. Why did they have to have such experiences? I looked at my own life, my experiences. Yes there were some larger than papers—a close friend now dead, divorce, bills, and debilitating diseases. This doesn't make sense! This world doesn't make sense and God doesn't make sense!

It doesn't make sense that God told Noah to build an ark, but . . .

Noah did everything just as God commanded him . . . for forty days the flood kept coming on the earth, and as the waters increased they lifted the ark high above the earth. The waters rose and increased greatly on the earth, and the ark floated on the surface of the water . . . Every living thing on the face of the earth was wiped out; men and animals and the creatures that move along the ground and the birds of the air were wiped out form the earth. Only Noah was left and those with him in the ark. Genesis 6:22; 7:17–18, 23

. . . Noah and his family were saved by God's grace in the midst of sin's destruction.

Death and war are uncertainties in the world. My future appears an uncertainty before me. Why must life be so uncertain?

Paul, in Romans 5:3b–5, tells us to "rejoice in our sufferings, because we know that suffering produces perseverance; perseverance, character; character, hope. And hope does not disappoint us, because God has poured out his love into our hearts by the Holy Spirit, whom He has given us." Rejoicing in suffering? This doesn't make sense.

God doesn't make sense.

GOD GIVES US COMFORT AND HELPS US

GROW FROM
LIFE'S EXPERIENCES.

It doesn't make sense that bread and wine are also body and blood, but . . . "Jesus took bread, gave thanks and broke it, and gave it to His disciples, saying, 'Take and eat; this is My body.' Then He took the cup, gave thanks and offered it to them saying, 'Drink from it all of you. This is My blood of the covenant, which is poured out for many for the forgiveness of sins.'" Matthew 26:26–28

God gives us a gift—the forgiveness of sins.

It doesn't make sense that a Father would give up His only innocent Son and let Him be beaten, bruised, laughed at, nailed to a tree, and die but . . .

For God so loved the world that He gave His one and only Son, that whoever believes in Him shall not perish but have eternal life. John 3:16

. . . God the Father gave up His Son, Jesus, to pay for all of our sins, each and every one. He didn't deserve it, but He paid the ransom that through faith we may go to heaven and live with our Savior forever.

It doesn't make sense, we should have died eternally, but let's be thankful that some things just don't make sense.

Lord, sometimes life doesn't make sense. At the same time You are taking care of me and all of the world. You have everything under control. It doesn't make sense that Jesus came to die for me but He did. Thank You, Lord, for Your saving grace and that some things just don't make sense. In Your Precious Name. Amen.

REASSURANCE

Read: Romans 8:35–39

Like nearly every person alive on September 11, 2001, I remember exactly what I was doing. I was working at my campus job. I stood in my office with my coworkers glued to our television. We watched smoke billowing over New York and Washington, and we really didn't know what was going on. The university president and many high-ranking faculty members rushed into our office. They tossed about different options to comfort the students. I realized at that moment that everyone was scared, even people in charge, and that scared me even more. People were crying. Everyone just looked dazed. I stayed long enough to see the second tower fall, then I walked home. During my walk I remember thinking that this event would forever change the way my generation and I viewed the world. I was not ready for that reality. Would we always feel this fearful? Would the world ever be safe?

Life is scary. We have a nation and a world around us at war. We have terrorists threatening to kill massive numbers of people for no reason. We have people dying of hunger on our streets and the streets throughout the world. We have a worldwide AIDS epidemic and cancer that strikes our family members. We have crime, death, and illness surrounding us. This is the life we know. It is not a pretty world. It is sin at its worst.

So what is the answer to sin in our world? On September 14, at the memorial service President Bush gave the country, the world, the greatest comfort that can be given. He quoted a passage from Romans 8.

Who shall separate us from the love of Christ? Shall trouble or hardship or persecution or famine or nakedness or danger or sword? As it is written: "For your sake we face death all day long; we are considered as sheep to be slaughtered." No, in all these we are more than conquerors through Him who loved us. For I am convinced that neither death nor life, neither angels nor demons, neither the present nor the future, nor any powers, neither height nor depth nor anything else in all creation will be able to separate us from the love of God that is in Christ Jesus our Lord. Romans 8:35–39

There is nothing, absolutely nothing that can separate us from God's love—not crashing towers, burning rubble, terrorists, or even fear. With His death on the cross, Christ conquered all—even death. So when you find yourself in doubt over the state of the world and a God that "seems" to control it, remember He *is* in control. Yes, there is terrorism, death, hunger, and unexplained illness, but that does not mean God has left His creation. It only means that this world is merely where we wait to go to our real home—our heavenly home—the place God prepares for all whom He has brought to faith. Jesus promised His disciples before His crucifixion: "In this world you will have trouble. But take heart! I have overcome the world," (John 16:33b). He gives us the same promise. Yes, world, members of this generation and future generations, take heart;

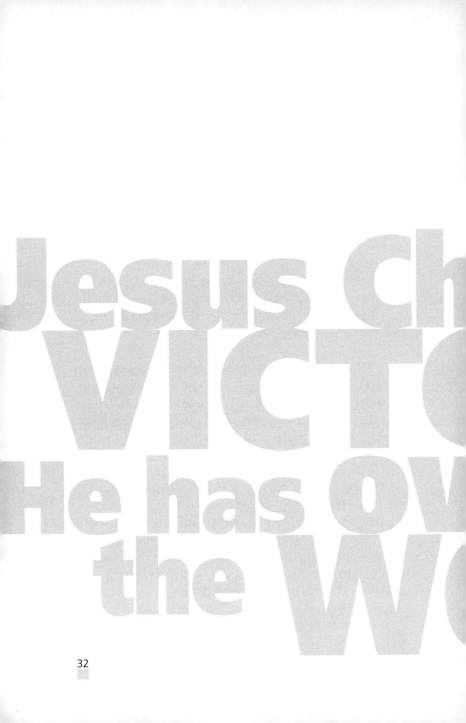

Jesus Ch
VICTO
He has OV
the W

Dear Lord, thank You for the gift of Jesus Christ. Through His death on the cross He has conquered the world. When we are prone to worry and despair because of evil in the world, give us the strength to lean on the promises of your Word and proclaim Christ's victory as our only true hope. In His name we pray. Amen.

ONE LOST SHEEP

Read: Matthew 18:1–14

After high school, living on your own or at college, it is easy to feel like a lost sheep in a great big world. The world is large, bills fly at you, assignments pile up. The world is your pasture—eat up!

Christ calls us His sheep. That probably doesn't mean too much to you. You may have never even seen a sheep. You may simply know that a sheep is a barnyard animal that goes "BAHHHH." Well the comparison goes further than that.

Sad to say, if we are sheep, it is not looking good for us. You see, sheep are pretty dumb animals. They have been domesticated for thousands of years (way back into Moses' time). They are not a "super hero" animal. They are weak; they don't have sharp teeth, fangs, or tough skin. Worse yet they are fairly slow animals in comparison to predators. They eat the grass that grows; what this means is they are not hunters. And because they have been domesticated for so long, it is next to impossible to set them free into the wild and expect them to survive. Sheep also have a tendency to follow the pack. Sound familiar? Are you feeling a little like a sheep yet?

What sheep need is a shepherd. Surprise! Jesus calls Himself our Shepherd. Just as a shepherd loves and protects his herd, Christ loves and protects us. He leads us to "quiet waters" (Psalm 23:2b). This is both literal and figurative. He provides for our every need, but He also gives us the comfort and peace of quiet waters.

Not the most perceptive, we sheep have the tendency to wander. Sheep can wander right off a cliff. That's smart. Well friends, we are like that too. We will wander away from God—straight to our death. Thanks be to Christ, our Good Shepherd, who keeps a watchful eye on us.

Those late teens and twenties years are a time of wondering. It can be lonely. We can feel like a lost sheep, not knowing which direction to take, lacking a leader we can follow. Like sheep, we are excited to graze, excited to experience the world and its green pastures, but wandering can lead us to unseen cliffs. We have a shepherd who promises to guide us. He promises to take care of us. To feed us, protect us, and, although our minds are small, to love us anyway.

At the end of the parable of the lost sheep we find that the loving shepherd leaves his 99 sheep in search of 1 lost sheep. Now you are a smart adult. Talk about poor economics on the shepherd's part. He could easily lose a pack of 99 sheep, yet he comes after his one lost sheep. He comes after *you*! You, His child, lost, but you, His child, is found, and He rejoices after *you*! "Your father in heaven is not willing that any of these little ones should be lost" (Matthew 18:14). Jesus loves you, His little sheep. College is a time when straying from the fold happens before we realize it. No matter what we have done or how far we have strayed, God is there welcoming us back. As we approach Him with repentant hearts, we can be assured that our heavenly Father, our Good Shepherd, will be there welcoming us back into the fold.

Dear Lord, I am a dumb sheep who has the tendency to wander. I am sorry for the times I have strayed from You. Thank You for Christ, my Good Shepherd, who brings me back into His heavenly fold. Thank You for the gift of Jesus' death and resurrection, which covers the sins of *all* people, especially mine. In Jesus' name. Amen.

RECONSTRUCTION

Be kind and compassionate to one another, forgiving each other, just as in Christ God forgave you. Ephesians 4:32

PURIFIED THROUGH CHRIST

Read: Ephesians 5:25b–27

Dorm life. It's different from home. New rooms, new showers, shared bathrooms, new food, new people. You bring with you your array of Target dorm room decorations—bright colors on everything and anything under the sun. Mom, afraid you will starve away from her stove, sends you off with all but the kitchen sink in terms of kitchen utensils, cleaning products, baked goods, canned goods, and every type of food that promises preparation in under five minutes. You may wonder why you even have some of these things in your boxes as you unload them into your tiny dorm room. For apartment dwellers, you get a bit more space, but not to worry, parents fill it up with an even greater array of fix-it tools and Easy Mac.

One such odd item I found myself owning was a water purifying pitcher—a handy tool for counteracting Chicago's "tasty" lake water. While an odd item for an already packed small fridge, it came in very useful as I adjusted to the different water. Smelly, sour water was transformed into clear, pure, odorless, tasteless liquid. The filter has an amazing system of tightly packed sand that when water is poured through it becomes clean.

Often times I see my life like that water pitcher. Filtered. All that I do looks like dirty water. It is smelly, dirty, and no matter how nice the crystal glass it is poured into, it remains unpleasant to drink. Like Jeremiah 2:22 tells us, no mater how much soap and scrubbing, the stain still lingers. Yet, through the filter, my actions can have the pure quality of good water. My actions can become God-pleasing when filtered through Christ. Sanctified, through the blood of Christ and the waters of Baptism, we are a new creation. Like pure water, we don't have the traits of the old dirty form; instead we reflect Christ.

In Ephesians, Paul tells us of cleansing through the filter of Christ. Jesus, the husband of His Church, cleanses it. He purifies you and me! He presents us to God as pure creatures "without stain or wrinkle or any other blemish, but holy and blameless" (Ephesians 5:27). We are holy, stainless, pure creatures only through the filter of Christ's blood. What an amazing image: cleansed through blood.

Like the pitcher, which had to be refilled every day, we need that sanctification every day. Jesus' death and resurrection won for us our justification under the law. Our debt is paid. Yet, like the faucet that I turned on each day, unclean water came out. Each day the pitcher had to be filled. We are sanctified, but the purification goes on each day in our drowning of the Old Adam. In this way we remember our Baptism and what God does for us—cleanses us from sin.

> Dear Lord, thank You for the purification process through which I experience each day in Jesus. Thank You for forgiveness, for justifying me by Your grace through the death and resurrection of Your own Son. Help me to live each day as Your child. In Jesus' name. Amen.

ROBE

Read: Colossians 3:1–17

What you wear in college matters. Yeah, everyone tells you that you can go to class in pajamas and you never have to wear more than shorts and a T-shirt. As a result, whenever someone thinks of a college student, they usually envision a grungily clothed and greasy haired overgrown teenager. Dressing down is a benefit of college, yet it still has its time and place. For instance, while it may be okay to wear pajamas to class on a regular day, it is not okay to wear pajamas on the day of your formal senior presentation.

As Christians, we find the same law at work in our spiritual lives. We are called to be clothed with "compassion, kindness, humility, meekness, and patience." But when we put on our fresh face of kindness in the morning, by bedtime it is a marred ruined mess. On our own, we are unable to do these things. When we look in the mirror of the Law at our clothes, we see only dirty rags hanging from our bodies.

Yet there is hope because Christ became human so He could fit His perfect white robe to us. He then freely gave us that robe so God would see us as Him, not as the sinful people we are. Our dirty rags are turned into His glorious white robe as John tells us in Revelation:

> Then one of the elders addressed me saying, "Who are these, clothed in white robes, and from where have they come?" I said to him, "Sir, you know." And he said to me, "These are the

—IN MORE THAN JUST A BATHROBE

ones coming out of the great tribulation. They have washed their robes and made them white in the blood of the Lamb." Revelation 7:13–14

Through daily repentance and forgiveness, we are daily clothed in these robes. As Martin Luther explains in his small catechism, through daily repentance we experience daily forgiveness. God thus daily dresses us in clean clothes and gives us the chance to be witnesses for Him.

It does matter what a person wears, especially a Christian. When clothed in our own works we are despicable, but when clothed in Christ we have been purified and granted new life, a chance to join the throng for the wedding feast of Christ and His bride, the Church. In Christ, we are clothed in those things Paul exhorts us to be clothed in: "compassion, kindness, humility, meekness, and patience." His attributes are given to us that God might see us as Christ, not the sinful body of the old Adam. Freely clothed in Christ, we live for Christ as Christ would have us live. To Him be all glory, now and forevermore.

Heavenly Father, in sending Your Son to become human flesh, You made Him the new Adam with whom I am to clothe myself. Give me His robe of righteousness and clothe me in His flesh that I might spend eternity in heaven with the saints. Through Jesus Christ our Lord. Amen.

TOO MUCH BASEBALL?

Read: 1 Samuel 16:7b

I was so excited to go to college—to be on my own, away from my family, living semi-independently. A new chapter in my life was starting and I couldn't be happier to begin it in a wonderful Christian environment where I knew my faith would mature. But you see . . . I had forgotten something. In my eagerness to choose a school, I looked at all my basic requirements: tuition, dorms, the quality of the education, the Christian environment. That was all there at Concordia University, River Forest. I guess the part I forgot was that I was from St. Louis . . . and would be living in Chicago for a good ten months. Don't see the connection? Think baseball. The St. Louis Cardinals and the Chicago Cubs have a decades-old rivalry that is generally friendly. But at school, I experienced the . . . um . . . not-so-friendly side.

I was cursed at downtown when I happened to be wearing a Cardinals cap. People gave me strange looks and of course had a *huge* chip on their shoulder. (I can't help it if the Cardinals have won nine World Series and the Cubs have only won two!) Worst of all, random people I didn't know would come up to tell me that the Cardinals lost. It was horrible. I wanted to go back to the familiar: my house, my family, and the city I had lived in for eighteen years of my life. Cubs' fans were not loveable losers. They were annoying and, frankly, it made me mad.

Then one night, early in my freshman year, I learned a lesson. I ended up sitting down and having this amazing discussion with an acquaintance. I am not sure exactly how we were thrown together, but there was an instant connection—we felt comfortable around each other immediately. We talked about our family, our future goals, and, most important, our faith. It was such a faith-affirming discussion and by the time we both left, I knew that God had placed a new, encouraging friend in my life. As I turned back to say goodnight, I seriously almost swallowed my own tongue. There was my new friend putting on a *Chicago Cubs* baseball hat. And with a sick feeling in my stomach I admitted to myself that if I had seen the hat at our initial hello, there would have been no discussion. Honestly, there might be no friendship today. I would have avoided him like the plague.

1 Samuel tells us that when God looks at us, He's looking at something completely different. Humans look at clothes and hairstyles, sometimes even skin color or size. We simply look at what is in front of us and then judge so shallowly. Sometimes we even turn away because of a Cubs hat. Aren't you thankful that when God looks at us He sees our heart? He doesn't judge us by our selfish actions or our hurtful words. Even better, when He gazes into our heart, it is with the eyes of a Savior. He sees a heart that loves Him, a heart saved through grace. If our Creator can look past our disgusting and sinful nature to see the heart underneath, wouldn't it be nice if we learned from that? Look past the outward—the frivolous and often misunderstood—and yearn to get to know and understand the inward. God will have some amazing hearts waiting for you.

Dear Lord, It amazes me everyday that You were willing to pay for my sins, to create in me a clean heart. I thank You that You see that renewed heart in me. I need Your help in putting aside my fear so I am able to see people as you do. Thank You for placing the gift of a godly friend in my life. In Christ's name. Amen.

RINSE CYCLE

During my freshman year of college, one of the first things I had to get used to was doing my own laundry. Sure, I had done laundry at home, but doing laundry in a dorm was a whole new experience. For one thing, I had to have really good timing. I had to know when to drag all of my dirty laundry down several flights of stairs to a dimly lit basement and hope that at least one washing machine was available. Laundry at college also cost money, which was yet another hardship to having clean clothes in college. It's no wonder that many people walking around a college campus generally have grungy, wrinkled looking clothing.

You arrive at college, boxes filled with fresh clean clothes. And before the end of the week you will have a pile of dirty clothes.

College is a time when a lot of people do a lot of laundry—physically and spiritually. College is a fresh start to begin making a dent in a laundry bag that for some is already very large. It's a bag filled with missteps, thoughtless words, hurtful actions, and a variety of other problems. It can be a bag filled with poor choices, bad relationships, addictions, premarital sex, lies, and laziness. So often it feels like we just keep adding to the bag another piece of clothing, another sin, another habit. Soon we find ourselves judged by the dingy clothes we wear. "She has dirty clothes coming out of her closet." "His entire room is a pile of dirty laundry." If you never were one to fold your clothes or make your bed, college is a place you can start. Yes, those freshly washed sweaters and shirts will get dirty, and so will your actions. It is inevitable. But with God's help, habits can be changed, life patterns can change.

When I do my laundry at school, I try to get every last item in the washers. I always return to my room to find one dirty sock. Yes, on our own, we can never free our lives from sin. Isn't it refreshing to know that there is a heftier, stronger, ultra of the ultras detergent that can wash our sinful lives. Christ. Christ in His blood washes us from the grime and nasty odor of sin.

Although we fail at "laundry," as all people do, we know that we have help. Christ's death on the cross eliminated our laundry list. Every day we can take out a new self through Baptism, free from stains and smudges, and wear it with the knowledge that we are freed from sin. Even sins that stain as deep as scarlet can be removed and made white.

> Dear Lord, thank You that Jesus' death on the cross has removed the stain of sin from our lives. Help us to remember His sacrifice as we begin each day freed from the tarnish of sin. In Jesus' name. Amen.

FREEBIE

Read: Isaiah 53:4–10 and Romans 3:23–24

Getting things for free is an exciting thing. Sometimes companies give out free things as a way of advertising. We may not need the candy, posters, cups, or other such items that are being handed out, but when someone is giving them away for *FREE,* we are happy to take them. At college there are dozens of "free" resources: clubs, study sessions, and materials. Maybe it was after taking your first economics course, or maybe it was long before this, that you found out little in life is really free. Oftentimes we find we are paying for the item that was supposedly "free." We come to understand that the free sample of shampoo or poster is budgeted into advertising and we pay for it later in the cost of the product. Or you find out that the university uses part of your tuition and fees to pay for the "free" resources it offers.

As we look around to see a world dominated by economic realities, we are tempted to see God in the same light, thinking our perfection or our good works could buy our salvation. But this is not the case. God gives us His grace *freely.* It is a free gift, no strings attached! We can do nothing to earn our salvation. We are imperfect—sinners. But God still wants us to be saved. That's why God gives us salvation freely.

The thing we need to remember is that this grace was not free. God gave the most precious thing He had to pay for our sins: His Son. Jesus came into the world and lived a perfect life. He took the sins of the whole world and paid the ultimate price by dying on the cross for them.

He died a horrible and gruesome death. He was beaten and whipped, taunted and spit on, falsely accused, and unfairly tried. With a broken and bleeding body, He was forced to carry His cross. Then, on the cross, Christ died our death, our payment, so we might have a free gift. This gift lasts for all eternity.

In our day-to-day lives, it's sometimes easy to take for granted what Christ did for us. As God, Jesus could have come down from the cross any time. Instead, He willingly laid down His life out of love for us. He paid the debt of all our sins so we can spend eternity with Him. What an amazing gift! We have the assurance that no matter how bad our day is, Christ is there with us, He knows what we're going through and He will *never* forsake us or leave us.

God gave this free gift, not only to us, but to everyone in the world. This gives us the opportunity to share God's grace with all the people around us each and every day. This is a "freebie" that we will want to share with everyone. Show people the best gift we have: the grace of God through Jesus!

Heavenly Father, thank You so much for the free gift of Your Son, Jesus Christ and the grace and salvation You gave us through Him. Help us to daily remember the sacrifice Christ made for us, and to share this wonderful message with others. In Jesus' name. Amen.

MUCH FORGIVEN

Read: Luke 7:36–50

A broken relationship, a semester of poor grades, selfishness, stupidity, partying, lust, ignoring God, and blazing my own trail, the list went on. The semester—the past year—my friend recounted it all to me. I knew it. I had been there with her. I knew how hard it had been on her and I knew what she had been suffering from—guilt. We talked over a latte at the coffee shop. She was depressed and in need of comfort—true comfort. I listened and comforted, but they were only words. I was there on a weekend visit and didn't know what I could do or say in one night to make it all better. Sunday morning we went to church with our friends and there, I found the answer when I least expected it. God sent His answer in His Word.

The Gospel that day was Luke 7:36–50. Jesus teaches an unforgettable lesson of forgiveness to His disciples and the sinful woman. *For he who has sinned much, there is much forgiveness.* Jesus shares a story of a man who cancels two debts, one small and one large. Jesus points out that the happier of the two is the one with the larger debt. Logical isn't it? When you owe a lot and are worrying about how to pay for it, you will be all the more happy if the banker says "Forget it, don't worry about it." But Jesus doesn't use the word "happy," He uses the word "love." Well of course you are thinking, "I would love the guy too, if he cancelled my debt."

The woman was not in debt though; with a large vessel of perfume she had money. But with her profession and history, she had a debt of another kind—sin and guilt.

At times, we are all like that woman; we look at our histories and see a debt of sin. Maybe we are not prostitutes by profession, but by our sinful human nature we have spiritually prostituted ourselves. At times we see our lives as mounds of sin, piled so high we don't know how to get around it. We look at our lives, the ones we try to control, the ones we find ourselves messing up and wonder, why would God love me? My debt is too big to cancel. But this is the beauty of the Lord. He canceled all—*all* sin on the cross. Even those who have sinned much have been given much. They have been given God's grace and forgiveness.

Paul reminds us that although God has given us grace, we do not sin all the more to have grace abound. In love we desire to serve Him. When we fall and see the walls of sin looming high over us, we know we have a ladder out of the deep well of our sin. We have Christ whose waters of Baptism wash us clean of that sin.

> Dear Lord, at times I find myself surrounded in my own sin. I am overwhelmed at what I have done in my life. I despair at my condition. Thank You for canceling my sin on the cross. Please give me the peace and love of the canceled debt. In Your name I pray. Amen.

LETTING GOD GUIDE

Read: Romans 5:1–2

Josh lived in California. He loved to hang with his friends and chat with girls at the beach, but most of all he loved tennis. When he was a freshman, he went out for the boy's tennis team. His high school had just come off its fourth straight state title. Despite his uncertainty, Josh made the team.

Josh arrived at practice to find himself paired up against Matt. Matt was a senior, the team captain and the number one player in the state. Josh felt his entire body go numb as he slid onto the court and prepared to play. Coach sat down on court one as Josh began practice across the net from the state's premier player. Matt hit every ball with ease, but Josh struggled to hit the ball at all. This pattern continued for the first week of practice. Every night Josh would practice for hours at a time still trying to fix his mistakes, but it was no use. Josh went to Coach Jones' office at the beginning of the second week of practice with his head hung in resignation, thinking for sure that coach had made a mistake picking him for the team.

"I'm sorry, Coach. I don't know what's wrong. But please let me stay on the team. I'll try harder, I promise." "Josh, nobody is taking you off the team," Coach said. "You earned your spot and you don't have to try to be like everyone else. You're just a first year player on this team. These other guys have been through this and know what it takes to be good. Just relax and play tennis like you know how. Okay?" Josh nodded his head and left.

The next week of practice went much more smoothly for Josh. He began to hit the ball better and soon found himself back in his rhythm. His nervousness was no longer there. He was just himself—part of the team.

Many Christians find it hard to believe they are new creations in Christ. They think they have to try harder and do better to gain the identity they've already been freely given. Do you find yourself trying harder or "performing" to feel valuable or loved by God?

This is a great example of what it's like to be part of God's family. When we become part of His family, we strive to be the perfect Christian. But since perfection is impossible, we find ourselves discouraged. When we try to be a perfect Christian on our own, we will always fail. We can never succeed without the help of God. When we fail, we need to realize that no matter what we do, God freely offers forgiveness through Jesus Christ, and that the Holy Spirit will continue to guide and direct us in our daily walk.

Dear Jesus, I ask for Your guidance and direction. Help me to see Your leading in my life. By the power of the Spirit strengthen me for my daily walk of faith. In Jesus. Amen.

JUST THE THING FOR *IT*

Read: John 20:21–23

You did it, and now it's done. Too bad there's no undoing it or redoing it. Much as you wish it wasn't, done is done. But now you can't get rid of it. That's the problem. It won't go away. Hanging about your neck like a noose pulling in the wrong direction, there's no shaking it. To say that it is weighing you down is a grandiose understatement.

"What is it?" is a question that only a small minority of folks can honestly ask, and that minority is likely lying. If you think that you can honestly ask, "What is *it*?" then you can skip the rest of this devotion. You know what *it* is. God knows what it is, and you and God both know that it is wrong.

You've done it. You may still be doing it. It may even be habitual. And you can get no rest. Perhaps you've tried to talk to a friend about it. They likely tried to make you feel better, perhaps trying to get you to forget about it for awhile, or by comparing your it to someone else's so it wouldn't seem so bad. I don't need to tell you that you're getting sugar water when you are in need of real medicine.

And if you could shake it or the scar it has left, you would have done so by now. But you can't. Your Baptism wiped it clean originally, but now it's back. Even confessing it, again and again, silently—secretly—is doing no good.

Jesus died for it. He doesn't want to see it around

your neck. He wants it in *His* nail-scarred hands. What is missing in this picture is simply the time and place where Jesus takes it off your shoulders, off your conscience. That time and place, your drop-off point, His pick-up point, are Confession and Absolution.

The beauty of John 20:21–23 is that Jesus sends certain people to forgive sins, in this case His disciples. Jesus reaffirms what we already know, namely that we can't get rid of our its by ourselves, not with our prayers, not even with our good resolutions. But Jesus too wants it gone, and therefore He empowers His people to forgive sins. Forgiveness happens when and where they forgive sins. Then and there all its become nothings. Jesus' forgiveness is absolute. That's Absolution.

Ready to be rid of it? There's no need to fear. No pastor may ever mention any its to anyone. When Jesus says, "I forgive you all of your sins—yes, even it," then it is gone. And gone is gone! Then you will be free, likely weeping tears of joy, able to breathe, lightened, alive, a new world before your eyes—forgiven. That is Absolution. Forgiveness is nothing less than all of that.

> O Lord Jesus Christ, who bid Your disciples to forgive and retain sins, grant that I may not be held back from going to my pastor, that my sin too may be forgiven, even as You live and reign with the Father and the Holy Spirit. Amen.

REMEMBERING

The LORD is a refuge for the oppressed,
a stronghold in times of trouble.
Those who know Your name will trust
in You, for You, LORD, have never forsaken
those who seek You. Psalm 9:9–10

Read: Exodus 4:1–17

When I left for college, I NEVER expected . . .

Life-long friends could be made the first day on campus.

A bag of burnt popcorn could fill a whole dorm with stench.

Prank wars and water guns could be so dangerous.

Finally making it home for break and seeing your family could induce joyous dancing.

Taking bloodied and bruised friends to the ER, without parents or adults, would be part of the job requirements.

Avoiding the unrecognizable cafeteria food would lead to eating day old un-refrigerated pizza.

How quickly strangers could become family.

Tired would be the perpetual state of everyone, even people who get lots of sleep.

People don't change; they just become more like themselves.

You can never anticipate what you are going to be asked to do in this life, especially not at college. There are going to be times when you will be faced with situations you never dreamed would come your way. Sometimes, the solutions to these situations are simple and even pleasant. Other times, however, the situation calls for something you won't believe you can do. It can stretch your talents and abilities. It can make you uncomfortable and nervous. Moses was called to one of those not so simple tasks himself.

In Exodus 4:1–17, God conversed with Moses from the burning bush, telling him to go to the Israelites and Pharaoh to bring His people out of Egypt. For an ex-royal who had run away from home and was living in the desert, this is a sticky situation. Moses wasn't expecting a burning bush or conversation with God, and definitely not to be the person expected to bring God's people out of slavery. So Moses did what any of us would do when faced with a situation that goes beyond our comfort zone. He questioned God's judgment. Moses asked God, "What if they don't believe me? I can't do it." So God gave Moses some amazing gifts, like turning his staff into a snake and water into blood as a sign that God was with him and would provide for him every step of the way. Then God did Moses one better. He gave Moses an assistant; God sent Aaron to go with him.

What do we learn from Moses? We may not be ready to deal with what comes our way, but God isn't going to leave us to deal with challenges by ourselves. God will show you gifts you never thought you had, and He will provide you with people to support you when you struggle. No matter what comes your way, you will not be left empty-handed and lost. God will provide what you need.

Dear heavenly Father, I know there are going to be difficult and trying times ahead, but I know that no matter what happens, You are never going to leave me. I ask that You bless me with whatever I need to do Your will in all situations. Thank You for helping me when I would fail on my own. In Jesus' name I pray. Amen.

WHERE NOW?

Read: John 6:28–29

Now what? You made it this far; graduation was the light at the end of the tunnel. Surprise! There are more tunnels ahead. Which way to go? Some go to college, but what should you major in? Which college should you go to? Maybe you should just skip college and get a job. What should you do for a living, then? Even if you think you have it all planned out, you never know when that curve ball will be thrown to turn your plans upside-down. If only there was a way to know what God wanted you to do in life. A neon sign, perhaps, that specifically stated what college, what major, what job, what spouse, what city, and what automobile you should choose. Then you would be set.

The Jews were asking "now what?" at the time of Jesus. Many thought He would be the political Messiah who would overthrow the Roman government. Instead, He ended the people's lifelong struggle to live up to the demands of the Law. Jesus said, "Do not think that I have come to abolish the Law or the Prophets; I have not come to abolish them but to fulfill them" (Matthew 5:17). The Law was all the Jewish people had known for thousands of years, and now this Jesus said that He fulfilled it in one lifetime? They were probably thinking, "Now what? If You fulfilled the Law, what do we do now if we want to do God's work?"

Jesus didn't give them a Law answer though. He told them one thing: believe. No more "do this" or "don't do that." To make God happy, just believe in the one He sent,

Jesus Christ, Himself. And you don't even do this yourself. As Martin Luther wrote, "I cannot by my own reason or strength believe in Jesus Christ, my Lord, or come to Him; but the Holy Spirit has called me by the Gospel, enlightened me with His gifts, sanctified and kept me in the true faith" (Luther's Small Catechism, p. 15).

What does this have to do with you? Well, if you're looking for a solid answer as to what to do with your life, look elsewhere. The thing is, wherever you go, you are doing what God wants when you remember the words of Christ: "Believe in Him whom He has sent." You shouldn't worry about whether or not you are really where God wants you because you are where God wants when you are in a place where you can proclaim the Gospel of Jesus Christ and have faith in Him. In the meantime, God will take care of calling you to the right place. Janitor or doctor, anyone is doing God's work when they have faith in Jesus. We have the words of Christ behind us, and that's more trustworthy than any neon sign.

> Lord Jesus Christ, You gave Your sure Word when You said that everyone who believes in You will have eternal life. Give us saving faith through the Holy Spirit, that we might proclaim Your Good News on all our paths in life. Through Your holy name we pray. Amen.

PLEASE SIR, MAY I HAVE SOME MOR

Read: Matthew 6:25–34; 7:7–11

One major reality for college students is money. For me, it decided whether or not I went to the University of Iowa. The summer after my freshman year my financial aid package was not what my family and I had hoped for. There was some grant money, but most of the $23,100 I needed had to be covered by student loans. I prayed hard and called financial aid. They gave me yet another student loan and knocked that amount off my parent's loan. But the amount the university expected of my parents was still way beyond their means.

My mom and I started to think about what to do if I couldn't go back to Iowa. I felt like I was dying inside. At the university I had found a great church, wonderful Christian friends, and a place where I really felt challenged. Needless to say, I did a lot of crying. I even wrote a letter to the financial aid office explaining our circumstances.

While I verbally professed that God would provide, I still doubted sometimes. I knew God promised to take care of all our anxieties, but I kept taking the financial ones back from Him. I thought it was my job to figure it all out. I forgot God's promises to provide; I doubted His ability to do so. We all struggle with doubting God's promises. We worry although we have been assured our Heavenly Father will provide all we need.

On the cross Jesus took our worries, fears, and doubts upon Himself. In the ultimate expression of God's grace, mercy, power, and might, Jesus gave His life for us and then rose again. We can cast our cares on Him because He's already taken them upon Himself. Through Jesus, the Father provides an outlet for worry and fear, He forgives our doubts, and He provides us with everything we need.

One day my mom announced there was a letter from Iowa. I jokingly said, "Well maybe they're sending me some free money!" I opened it up and on the top saw the words "Revised Financial Aid Statement." I had trouble locating the actual change, but then I saw it: "Tuition Scholarship, $3,692! Parent Loan, $7,070!" I started crying and hugged my mother. I had gone to the depths of despair and doubt, but God had lifted me out, demonstrating His great love for me and His power in my life. Had the money not come, I have no doubt that God's alternate plan for me would have been the right one.

Lord God, give us peace in all our worries, especially financial ones. Provide funds according to Your will and provide direction when the answer is "No." We praise You for all You provide for our every need. In the name of our Lord and Savior, Jesus Christ. Amen.

AND THE WAVES ROLL IN

Read: Ecclesiastes 3:1–8

You made the decision! It's one of the biggest decisions of your life. You used to wonder and maybe worry about what you would do after high school. But it's over. You decided to go to such and such university or college. "Ahhh," a sigh of relief.

I felt this way after making my college decision. I was relieved. However, I didn't realize what was coming. During my first semester I was faced with more decisions. For example, my career path, serious relationships, moral situations, and even how I will arrange my classes. At one point when considering my career choice, I said, "I don't know if I am undecided or not." Basically, I was confused.

At times of confusion or frustration I usually take a walk outside. My college campus is located on a bluff overlooking Lake Michigan. One night as I walked along the edge, I noticed some things about the lake. First, I could not see the entire lake, I could only see so far out. I wondered how large the lake really was and what was on the other side. Second, the sound drew my attention to the waves rolling up to the shore. One by one the waves came and then diminished. Then as I looked out onto the lake again I wondered if the waters farther out would eventually reach the shores as waves. The waters reminded me of my life and my relationship with God. Just as I could only see up to the horizon of the lake, I am limited in how much I know about my future. Furthermore, each wave represents an event in my life. Each wave and each event comes at its own time. Lake Michigan taught me a great lesson that night.

The most comforting fact is that God is in control of the waters. He sees the entire lake and makes the waves roll in. Even more, He created the lake. He also created you. He can see your entire life and knows when waves will roll into your life. He even plans the waves to come at just the right time. Ecclesiastes 3:1 reads, "There is a time for everything, and a season for every activity under heaven." I pray that as you enter college, career, or whatever, you are comforted in knowing your life is in the hands of God. He knows the timeline of your life and He will be there every step of the way guiding you as you make decisions.

> Dear Lord, please guide me as I make decisions in life and help me take comfort in knowing You can see my entire life and are in control of its timing. You are amazing! Amen.

CONVINCED

Read: Romans 8:38–39

I am certain I cried more tears the first six weeks of my college career than I did at any other time in my life. I was in a new place, away from home, with no friends, and to top it off, my boyfriend, who I was convinced was the love of my life, dumped me! I was positive my life had ended! I was convinced I would never find happiness again in anything! I was convinced that "college" was this cruel trick society played on young adults to keep us humble. I was convinced that my mom and dad sent me away to experience misery, and they had no desire to see me succeed or be happy. I was convinced about a lot of things, but mostly I was convinced I was alone and doomed to stay that way forever. I was wrong! I was not alone; lots of people were feeling the same way I was. Most importantly, though, God was with me.

In those first six weeks of college I became so focused on what *I* was doing and how *I* was feeling, that I quit focusing on God's unchanging and eternal love for me. In my sinfulness, I had pushed God aside, had convinced myself that neither He nor His love were big enough, powerful enough, or strong enough to pick me up out of the gloomy depths of my self-created misery. I was reminded of the words of my confirmation, Proverbs 3:5–6; "Trust in the LORD with all your heart and lean not on your own understanding; in all your ways acknowledge Him, and He will make your paths straight." Those verses didn't tell me to trust God when I had the time or when it felt right. They didn't tell me to trust God with part of my heart and reserve the rest of it for my pity party. I knew those verses told me to trust in the Lord will all my heart, to forget about my selfish misery, and to let God guide and direct my way. So why was it so hard?

I had a hard time trusting God because I had put aside the fact that God's love goes with all believers everywhere at all times. Despite my weakness, God loved me. Despite my attitude, God loved me. Despite my location, God loved me. Despite how I was feeling, God loved me. Despite my sinfulness, God loved me. There was nothing I could do to separate myself from the love of God. Nothing!

God's love for us is indeed bigger than the problems we encounter. Be convinced that His love surpasses time, location, age, and attitude. St. Paul tells us in Romans 8 he is convinced there is nothing, good or bad, in all of creation great enough to separate us from the love of God that in is Christ Jesus: not death, not life, not the present, not the future, not even college!

> Heavenly Father, I thank You for loving me. Hold me firmly in the grip of Your love, Lord, and remind me that neither death nor life, neither angels nor demons, neither the present nor the future, that nothing can separate me from Your love. Amen.

ON YOUR OWN

Read: Psalm 139

Being on your own is one of the coolest things about graduating. You go from having a set schedule that you must follow to being the one who decides what *you* will do. Whether you're in college, the military, working, living on your own, or living with family, you become a lot more independent after high school.

In some ways, it is exciting and liberating. You get to decide when you get up, when and what you will eat, and what you will do that day. You can change the way you look, dress, act, think, and feel. You decide, day-by-day, how you're going to live your life.

In other ways, being on your own is frightening and difficult. You miss special friends or family members. There is the stress of being responsible for your actions and the consequences that come with your decisions. When you have had a hard day, there may not be someone there to support you. When life's troubles come along, there may not be someone to help carry your load. Sometimes, you just feel very alone.

That's where the amazing power of God comes in. No matter how much we think we are "on our own", God is always with us. He knows every action and thought. As David said in Psalm 139:1–4, "O LORD, You have searched me and You know me. You know when I sit and when I rise; You perceive my thoughts from afar. You discern my going out and my lying down; You are familiar with all my ways. Before a word is on my tongue You know it completely, O LORD."

Isn't is amazing? Every second of every day, our heavenly Father is right there with us. Even if we're not sure where our lives are going, God does. "'For I know the plans I have for you,' declares the LORD, 'plans to prosper you and not to harm you, plans to give you hope and a future'" (Jeremiah 29:11). No matter how hard or troubling life gets, God is still in control. Even in our worst times, He is giving us countless blessings!

Sometimes it feels like no one knows what you are going through. This is *not* true of Christ. He came to earth and lived a human life; He was tempted just like we are. But He lived a perfect life. He is the spotless Lamb of God who willingly went to the cross for us. He conquered death and sin to redeem us and give us His righteousness.

Although at times you may seem alone, you have the assurance that our gracious God is right there with you giving you guidance, comfort, and strength for the day. He promises to never leave you (Matthew 28:20b). You always have Jesus who understands the struggles and hardships in your life, and who gave you salvation and eternal life.

> Thank You, Lord, for Your wonderful promise to be with me. Thank You for the grace You gave us through Christ. Help me, when I'm alone, let Your promises strengthen me and Your loving arms surround me. In Jesus' name. Amen.

Read: 2 Corinthians 6:18

Graduation date was approaching fast, only a few months, and I still didn't know where to go to college. But after prayer and considerations I finally chose Concordia University Wisconsin. With my parents living in St. Louis, I was going to be seven hours away from home . . . or so I thought.

God had a different plan. In June, my dad received a call to be a professor at Concordia Wisconsin. After lots of thought and prayer, he accepted the call in July, and my family moved to Wisconsin in August. I thought my August trip to Wisconsin would be a typical mini-van full of college supplies. Instead, there was an enormous moving van with all of my family's belongings.

Basically, my parents followed me to college. At first I hated having my parents so close. I was supposed to be on my own, not fifteen minutes away from home. I even tried to pretend my parents weren't there, but that led to living in a surreal world. Eventually, I faced reality and changed my perception of college to one that included my parents. Although I still have some mixed thoughts about the situation, I have seen numerous blessings as a result. God taught me to follow His plans and trust Him rather than rely on my own thoughts or ideas.

Most likely your parents will not follow you to college. This may be comforting or scary for you. Maybe you can't wait to leave or maybe you would love for your family to come with you. Either way, you have a Father who will continue to be with you. Your heavenly Father will never leave you.

This thought might be either scary or comforting for you as well. You might have plans of your own once you are away from home and are independent. Plans you may not want God to be involved in. However, even in times you don't want God around He will patiently be there ready to forgive. Overall, I find comfort in knowing He is around. When life gets crazy and stresses about homework, money, and friendships arise, He is there to ease the burden. 2 Corinthians 6:18 reads, "I will be a Father to you, and you will be My sons and daughters, says the Lord Almighty." You are a child of God, and you have a Father who will always be there whenever and wherever.

> Dear Lord, You are my Father. As I start a new chapter of life, I know You will be there with me. Thank You for being a forgiving, loving, and everlasting Father. In Your Son's name. Amen.

SUFFERINGS OF HOPE

Read: Romans 5:1–11

"We rejoice in our sufferings, because we know that suffering produces character; and character, hope" (Romans 5:3b–4). These words from Paul's letter to the Romans float back into my mind every time I sit at my computer hacking out yet another paper at 2:30 in the morning. This was a small portion of the verses my girlfriend gave me in a card to encourage me as I wrote papers at the end of my freshman fall semester. It was less than encouraging hearing that suffering through this paper was going to produce character, and what was more that I was supposed to *rejoice* in it. I was overwhelmed with this paper! (I now consider it "short" and "easy" in comparison to whatever I am writing these days). I missed the true comfort of these words. The passage goes on to tell why we can find comfort in rejoicing in our sufferings.

"And hope does not disappoint us, because God has poured out His love into our hearts by the Holy Spirit, whom He has given us. You see, at just the right time, when we were still powerless, Christ died for the ungodly" (Romans 5:5–6). While I am tempted to think that this forgiveness applies to my procrastination on the paper, or that I want to associate with an extension as I down yet another Mountain Dew or thick coffee, I am reminded that this forgiveness runs deeper. This forgiveness is the forgiveness for the present procrastination on my paper, the sins from today's fight, lustful thoughts, yesterday's complaints and covets, and tomorrow's selfishness. That love demonstrated on the cross was the forgiveness that we—weak and incapable sinners in action and in nature—desperately needed.

When Paul wrote this passage about rejoicing in one's sufferings, he didn't have in mind typing a paper; rather his mind was on persecution. Rejoicing in the midst of persecution of character, of life, of home, this is what Paul was more likely speaking of to Christians of Rome. Like the papers and assignments that are sure to follow those first few days and weeks of college, so are the persecutions and trials of being a Christian. Yet Paul reminds us of the hope we have. Reconciled in Christ's blood and death on the cross, we have the hope of heaven. And in this hope is peace of a far greater depth than that which is felt when the last line of the paper is written and the sigh of completion is given. It is the peace of a new-found relationship with God as we are transformed from enemies to children of God. Where suffering could be felt among the fight to maintain good character, or truth, rejoicing can occur as the truth of the depth of our Father's love for us is made known. It is a love for us that sacrificed His Son in order to adopt us as His children.

> Dear heavenly Father, thank You for the hope and peace that I have in You. Though suffering and persecution may occur in this world, please grant me the peace that comes in the understanding that I am Your child, forgiven and made clean on Calvary. In Your most holy name. Amen.

SECURITY BLANKET

Read: Jeremiah 29:11

Security. When we were little, it came in the form of a blanket. Exiting high school a young adult, security is no longer found in a 3x3 foot square. Surrounded by friends, it may come from a peer support group. Or maybe it comes from the college you are planning to attend or job you plan to work at.

Security Alert! No money. Who will you call? Mom and dad most likely. They are only a phone call away with bank account numbers and advice. Security Alert! Roommate problems. Will you talk to your RA or maybe your landlord, your commanding officer, other friends perhaps?

Where do you get your security? Who or what is the security blanket you fall back on? As Christians, we struggle over this question every day of our lives due to the constant tug between our sinful human flesh and our sanctified soul. The devil would like nothing better than to grab onto your soul when you're weak and vulnerable, when you are looking for a source of security. In your college walk, you will experience your fair share of down times, times when you need a bit of security in a new environment. You might become angry, frustrated, hurt, or disgusted when you feel insecure in the midst of new friends, new classes, new work, and new responsibilities. You might even blame God.

It may seem that all of your plans have been foiled— and they have. Sin spoils everything it touches. We desire pleasure, power, wealth, and self-advancement, but we are left high and dry.

At times like this it is great to know that our God is a faithful God who has a plan specifically for you! God's plan is the perfect life for you—filled with security and prosperity, not harm. God's plan is filled with hope and it becomes your future! God's plan is in you and you are in God's plan. God's plan is the plan of salvation that is in Christ Jesus. It began on Calvary with the words, "It is finished" and will end on the last day when we will see Him face to face. This plan is in you—it was given to you in your Baptism!

Along your college walk, your plans may fail, but remember that God's plan has your best interests in mind. It begins in the Word of God where you receive strength from God's words and promises! Praise the Lord for His plan of goodness and mercy!

> Heavenly Father, thank You for the plan You work in and through me. Forgive me when I think my plan will give me what I need and doubt that Your plan is sufficient. Keep me in Your Word so I may walk in Your plan! In Jesus' name. Amen.

ALL IN HIM

Read: Philippians 4:11–13

I recall reading this passage somewhere in October of my first year at college. I found myself lifted up by the words of Paul, who knew struggles. I was out of money, in need of a job, and unwilling to ask my parents for more. They were struggling with their own financial issues and the last thing I wanted was to be a burden. In addition my aunt was diagnosed with breast cancer, and my mind was distracted by one of my high school friends' problems. This was all piled on me, the lonely, confused freshman, struggling with all the issues of being a new student at a university far from all the reassurance of home.

I felt alone as I searched the job boards and plugged through the classes. Sure, I was surrounded by other students, even a floor full of freshman women with the same new experiences. But these new friends did not seem like the right people to handle *all* of the stuff going through my mind.

I read over this familiar passage in Philippians and it began to take on a new meaning for me. I had always heard people use this verse as a "glorified you-can-do-it." But as I read the surrounding verses, a new, more reassuring meaning glimmered through the words on the page.

I connected with Paul's statement, "I know what it is like to be in need" (verse 11). I was reminded of financial struggles and rough times growing up and the contentment of knowing that somehow we had made it. God always provided for us. I knew He promised to and I saw it happen. I was reassured that my situation would work out. But Paul and I had known different needs. The faith of Paul became apparent to me. Paul who struggled sharing the message of Christ, Paul who saw the inside of many a prison, who persisted despite the Roman decrees against sharing the Gospel, who dealt with persistent church problems. I felt silly complaining about a lack of money.

We may not all deal with the problems of Paul, but we do deal with the struggle to share our faith with our neighbors. We all deal with very real problems like money, illness, and poor choices. Yet, for Paul and for us, this need not be a struggle or even a reason to complain; rather it is a reason for contentment. Paul discussed the secret of contentment—Christ! Christ was his contentment in all situations. Sounds a bit too easy—right? It is the joy Christians have to be able to rejoice in the knowledge of a Savior whose death and resurrection has removed the *real* fear of eternal damnation. This is the joy: Christ. There is a peaceful contentment that comes with knowing God is in control. God will provide. He, not I, got me a job that year; He, not doctors, heals illness; He, not us, gives contentment.

Lord, give me the joy and comfort of knowing You are in control of my life. You, who can do all things, Lord, grant me freedom from worry, which I cannot fix as they are only Yours to heal. In Your name I pray. Amen.

SURVIVING SENIOR YEAR

or moving moun at the very least

Read: Matthew 17:20

I think it is reasonable to determine that at some point in their high school career nearly every student reaches a point when they simply cannot wait for their senior year. This enthusiasm is not due to some hereditary gene that is passed from one generation to the next, and is not bound by race, creed, or gender. It seems as though there is something extra appealing about being at the top in the brutal society known as high school. There's supposedly a mysterious respect and confidence you acquire when you become a senior. Of course, I never fed into any of that!

. . . Okay, so I'm lying. I was about as psyched as everyone else who entered school this year as a senior. Senior year meant carefree fun! Senior year meant special privileges! And while it does mean both these things to a certain extent, I was not prepared for the other things that senior year meant. Senior year means applying for tens— dare I say it—seemingly hundreds of colleges and scholarships. Senior year means being reminded about setting a good example for the underclassmen. For many of us, senior year means juggling several extracurricular activities, clubs, and challenging classes that will make us look good on the aforementioned college and scholarship applications.

Simply put, senior year is not all it's cracked up to be (a startled gasp goes up from the audience)! It's not all fun and games. In fact, there may be times when the fun and games part seems nonexistent.

So what do you do now? You've been counting down the days until your blessed first day of senior year. Or maybe you're already in the thick of senior year, with 70 scholarship applications in front of your face (because let's face it, that part-time job, that major English paper, and all those after-school chores are not enough for you to handle!). Is this any reason to be filled with dread? Of course not!

Before you throw this book across the room and slump hopelessly on the couch, relax! Take a deep breath; look up. Smile, not because your dad finally fixed that stubborn leak in the ceiling, but because your heavenly Dad is watching over you. He knows your troubles, He knows your ever-growing to do list, and He knows you are stressing. God won't turn His back on you because He loves and cares for you. That's His great promise!

Jesus tells us in Matthew 17:20 that with the gift of faith in God, we as mere humans can do anything! Even when we falter in our faith, which we as sinners have a tendency to do all too often, the tiniest amount of faith still allows us to move mountains. Whether you're a freshman who has just begun the venture through high school, a senior who is ready to finish the venture, or somewhere between, the blessing of faith from God will more than help you squeak by. Our God loves and cares for us so very much that He will sustain you through the stress and duties that lie ahead. By faith God can bless you with the time management skills to complete that English project, and maybe finish five or six of those college applications.

Congratulations! You just moved your first mountain.

Dear God, You know all of my burdens. You know exactly what I am going through. I know I can do anything with faith in You. Please help me keep my faith strong. Keep me focused on this year and the responsibilities I have. In Your most holy and precious Son's name I pray. Amen.

PLANS CHANGE

Read: Romans 8:28 and Proverbs 3:5–6

Choosing what you do after high school can be one of the biggest decisions of your life. That is how it was for me. College, which college? It was an important decision. I spent over a year poring over pamphlets, hunting through websites, and visiting colleges searching for where I would spend the next four years, the first years of my adult life.

So imagine my surprise when not even two months into the fall semester at the college of my choice, I wanted out. It had turned out to be a horrible misjudgment on my part. As early as the first week of classes, I decided I wanted to change my major. Imagine my dismay when I discovered this particular school didn't even offer the major I now wanted. Not only that, I hated being there. I wasn't making many friends. Overall depressed and lonely, I didn't want to admit I had made a mistake in selecting a college, but I couldn't ignore it either. Suddenly it seemed there was no other choice but to get out as quickly as I could.

I began searching the website of what had been my number two choice of schools. I especially looked into how easy it would be to transfer, and how quickly. I was never one for making snap, last minute decisions, especially not ones that essentially affected the rest of my life. This whole situation made me more nervous than I had ever been. My parents were quite surprised at my sudden desire to uproot and transfer schools so quickly, but they supported me 100%. It was yet another sign that this was the right thing to do. For the first time I really felt like I knew what God wanted me to do. That not only calmed my nerves but encouraged me to act more boldly than I ever had in my life.

From the first day at my new school, I knew God led me to the right choice. Everything I had worried about seemed to fall into place so perfectly that it seemed like God was telling me, practically shouting at me, that I was where I belonged. It didn't matter that I had wasted a semester; I learned things in that semester as well. The most important thing I learned was to trust God in all things, and He will take care of the rest. Not only am I more confident in myself and my future, but coming out of this experience also strengthened my faith and brought me closer to God.

Plans may change for you. But that's okay. God is there working good in whatever situation you are in. In all times, even in times of changing plans, God is there blessing your life.

Dear God, You and You alone know for certain what will be best for me in my life. Please guide and keep me as I make important choices and decisions that will impact my life. And in all things keep in my mind and heart that I do everything to Your glory. Amen.

DAILY BREAD

Read: Exodus 16 and Matthew 6:25–34

Oh, no! It was May; summer was here and still no job. I had hunted for a job and was still hunting. Nearly a month later I had one—part time. I crunched numbers and added and subtracted them again. I would just barely make the summer with living expenses and first month's rent. What about books? And then there was rent and living expenses for the fall?!

Since that summer, I have found the Lord working in mysterious ways. In little ways He reminds me that my worries are in His hands. That summer I learned the valuable lesson of daily bread. I was in college and struggling to be independent and failing every step of the way. I found myself worrying about my tomorrows and losing my todays.

In Exodus 16, the children of Israel learn the lesson of daily bread. Coming out of Egypt, they were used to having much to eat. In the wilderness they found themselves without food. They complained to Moses. The Lord provided, but not in the way they wanted Him to. He sent manna, an interesting dew-like substance, and quail. The fascinating thing was that although He provided for them, God insisted they rely on Him. He would not be insulted by their worry. If the Israelites tried to save their manna, it would rot and become infested with maggots. They were able to gather only enough manna for *that* day.

God tries to keep our wandering minds on today and its blessings. We, in our sin, focus on tomorrow and the unknowns. Matthew warns us about this. Focusing us on the fact that God has and will always provide for His people, Matthew points us to look at a lily. God gave it beautiful garments of color and so He will provide for our needs.

It is easy to fall into the trap of worry. You are, for the most part, on your own now, and that is scary. It can look like the earth is about to end when next semester's books need to be bought or rent is due and the checking account reads zero and the credit card is nearly maxed out. Parents, we love them, but it is hard to ask for money, and even harder to ask others. Jobs don't always pay enough. Life doesn't always work out the way we plan. But life always works according to God's plan. He is in control, providing for today. Tomorrow will come bringing more worries, no money, more rent due, and bills to pay. But that is tomorrow and this is today. God is here with us today and He will be there with us tomorrow too.

> God, give me the faith and trust that You have today under Your control and You have tomorrow too. Please take these worries
>
> _____ *(list worries)* _____
>
> _____
>
> _____
>
> _____
>
> into your care and guidance. Thank You for already having a plan to fix these things. In Your Son's name. Amen.

RE-EXAMINATION

Bear with each other and forgive whatever grievances you may have against one another. Forgive as the Lord forgave you. And over all these virtues put on love, which binds them all together in perfect unity. Let the peace of Christ rule in your hearts, since as members of one body you were called to peace. Colossians 3:13–15

PEACE

WHAT TO PACK

Read: Matthew 22:35–39 and 1 Corinthians 13

After the exodus from the not quite real experience of high school, you will enter the real world. For most of us this might mean we pack a bag or a carload and move out of our homes. We pack up our belongings, taking with us the most precious. If I could offer one piece of advice it would be about one thing to remember to pack—empathy—an acute sense of empathy.

A lot of the people I knew during my high school years, to say the least, had an underdeveloped sense of empathy. It showed through the most in how people dealt with those they did not particularly like, agreed with, understood, or simply even knew much about. It is part of who we are as humans. We tend to rush to judgment about other's motives, ideas, and actions. Yet, it is at these times we can hurt people the most without ever considering the effects we're having. Often we do not find out what they were dealing with in their life until many years later. It is then that you realize how much you hurt them.

I had an experience like this when I started at the Air Force Academy. We all thought "Joe" was pretty out there during our first few weeks of basic training, but after I got to know him during the school year, he ended up being one of my truest friends, and actually an incredibly talented musician.

So, how can you develop a sense of empathy? Like most things worthwhile in life, it is not attained overnight. You can start to understand where others are coming from and begin to imagine what life might be like for them only after you have given them a chance. In fact, it is more than a chance; you have to put effort into it. Consciously try to imagine all of the factors in their life on a given day, week, or even as a whole, and think how they might have changed your outlook on life. Would you really act much differently than they? However, it cannot stop at simply contemplating the complexity of their lives; it has to lead to change in how you treat them. This requires a considerably larger effort, as this requires a change in lifestyle. Maybe not always treating someone or acting in a way that is popular or easy, but instead helping those everyone else refuses to help. As I became better friends with the guy we thought was so out there during basic, I actually did end up losing some friendships, but at the same time made new ones that ended up being a lot less superficial.

The only way to really go about changing your empathy toward others is to realize it's not you. It's Christ. Christ died on the cross for *all* people. God's love and salvation is for you and me and all of the other people in the world. Through faith in Christ and in the study of His Word, empathy will spring up in you. In Matthew 22:37, when Jesus is asked which is the greatest commandant in the Law, Jesus responds, "Love." We are to love God completely and then love our neighbors second to God. Christ calls us to treat those around us as we treat ourselves. To love others is not only what Christ calls us to do, but without love, we are nothing. Without love, we cannot reflect Christ to others.

The greatest news is that God knows we can't love others or even Him on our own. So God gives us faith through His Spirit so we can be right with Him. As we grow in faith God strengthens us to love and serve others too.

Lord, I ask You to help me love my neighbors, to treat them as I would want to be treated. Grant me the patience and desire to look past the surface of others and understand them for who they are so my interactions with them and throughout my whole life can reflect You. In Your name I pray. Amen.

Cadet John Ethredge

AS THEY ARE

Read: Romans 15:1–13

I remember the first day arriving on campus. I met my roommate, quiet and shy; it looked like a tough year ahead. Then there were 12 other girls on my floor. I didn't know names then, but it looked scary. Two preppy girls wearing Gap clothing, one outspoken, the other dingy, on the one side of me was a loud girl and her roommate with a funny accent. There were a few others—nondescript. They all seemed nice enough. But none were like me. They were preppy or nerdy, talkative or quiet. The first impression was lacking something. I was let down because these girls were supposed to be my best friends for life, at least that's what I had always heard.

I am not sure when, but sometime that first week, some of those girls and I ended up talking late into the night about past relationships, likes and dislikes, jobs, college. The list ran on as our friendships grew over the coming months.

I learned a lot about first impressions and friendship. Now, three years later, I look at the girls I met that day, some close friends and others distant memories. To be friends, to love someone, you must first get to know them. Who they are, inside and out.

Paul talked about this in Romans when he said, "Accept one another" (Romans 15:7). It took getting to know the individuals on my floor to become friends with them. But I had to accept them where they were, or where I thought they were, in order to become friends with them. We could not open ourselves up to each other if we didn't drop the barriers of first impressions.

In this chapter in Romans, Paul discussed how to witness to others. Friendship, acceptance, was one way to share the Gospel with others. It "brings praise to God" (Romans 15:7) when we accept others as they are, weird, shy, preppy, nerdy, or whatever, and befriend them. This is an opportunity to share Christ with them. What a wonderful friendship it becomes when Christ is involved!

Dear Lord, please help me to see people as they are—Your children. Please help me to help and befriend them, and enable me to share You with them. In Jesus' name. Amen.

PSSSS...

GOSSIP

Read: Proverbs 26:20–23

Did you hear about Todd and Sheila?!?

How many times have you been in that situation? Whether you are giving out the latest tidbit of news or receiving it, you're gossiping. Sometimes, it's harmless, like a surprise birthday party. But most times, gossip ends up hurting someone. Sometimes the story may be true; sometimes not. No one stops and thinks, "Is this true? Would it hurt someone?" Reputations and friendships can be ruined by spreading such stories.

I once heard a story that illustrates what I'm trying to say here. A man had sinned against his pastor by spreading a story about him that wasn't true. He came to the pastor to beg for forgiveness. The pastor answered him by saying, "All right, I will forgive you; but first I'd like you to do something. I'd like you to take a pillow filled with feathers and climb way up to the top of the church steeple. Rip open the pillow and let the feathers fly to the ground." The man was confused, but he fulfilled the pastor's request. He came back after completing the deed and said, "I've done what you asked. Will you now forgive me for spreading that lie about you?"

The pastor said, "Certainly. But one more request. Gather up all the feathers that you just let go."

This story illustrates for us how once our words are out, we can never erase the impact they've had. Gossip is sin and it can hurt. It breaks God's commandments and destroys relationships. Yet we can find forgiveness for sin in the cross of Jesus. He died to forgive us and gives us strength to resist temptations, like gossip.

If you have been the object of some form of gossip, seek God's strength in Jesus to be restored. If you have a problem with gossip—stop sinning and go to the cross for forgiveness.

Next time a person approaches you with the latest gossip, don't believe everything you hear!

Lord, help me not to gossip about others. Let me look for the good in people and build them up instead of tearing them down. Help me set a good example for others. I ask this in Jesus' name. Amen.

IN COMPARISON

Read: Luke 18:9–14

Comparison. You know this word all too well. Your first day at college you meet your floor-mates and all you can think is *she is prettier than me, skinnier and she has nicer clothes. I know all of the guys are going to go for her.* Or guys, you may have already fought the guys on your floor to see who the alpha male is. We do it with our eyes, our thoughts, our words, and sometimes our strength. We envy what others have. This can come out in anger and resentment toward them, sometimes for things that aren't bad or even their fault.

Comparison can appear in other ways as well. We can look at others and rightfully or wrongly judge them. "He drinks every weekend and never does his homework," or "she sleeps around." To make judgments on other actions is hurtful. Not only could you have misinformation (let's face it, gossip is rampant wherever you go), but you could ruin another's reputation. Even thoughts like this are hurtful.

In Luke 18, Jesus tells a parable of the Pharisee and the tax collector. He describes comparison. The Pharisee compares himself to the tax collector. In the Roman world the tax collector would normally be a Roman, not a Jew, and looked down upon because they would steal from the people. It is easy to allow our witness to be like that of the Pharisee. To look down upon non-Christians; to say, and believe we are truthful when we say, we are better than them for it. We may believe that our actions are better ("I follow all of the commandments, or at least most, we all slip up here or there") or that we are better people ("I don't drink or smoke"). But these are all sinful lies we tell ourselves. These are lies that make us feel better about ourselves. We all know that a sin is a sin, regardless of which one it is. It is not a graded level of better or worse sins. Like the tax collector, we know that the payment for that sin is death. When God compares us to the Law, He sees not a mirror image but the greatest distortion. He sees a chart in the wrong direction. When He desires life, He sees death.

But there is hope; there is rejoicing. Where God saw no comparison, no equal payment for our sin on our behalf, He righted it. He offered for us His Son to make equal what we could not. Christ died on the cross to save us from our envy, our comparisons, our jealousy, our greed. He saved us from all sin. Thanks be to Christ for a sacrifice so great. "For by grace you have been saved, through faith and it is not from yourselves, it is a gift from God, not by works, so that no one can boast" (Ephesians 2:8–9). We are all under the same law. We have all sinned and fallen short of the glory of God. But thanks be to God for His glorious gift that goes beyond compare.

> Dear heavenly Father, I am sorry when I compare myself to others and when I judge them. Thank You for the gift of forgiveness of sins and salvation. In the name of Jesus I pray. Amen.

TRUE FRIEND

Read: Matthew 11:25–30

I was once told that a good friend will come and bail you out of jail after a night of hard partying, but a true friend will be in the cell next to you saying, "Man, that was fun." Such is the burden of true friendship, sharing in not only the glorious moments, but also the moments when life does not always go the right way. Picking up part of the load so your friend can still walk on.

Throughout college friendships wax and wane with the phases of the moon or the week of the month. Although you may try your hardest to keep a friendship alive and growing, it may collapse and fall into disrepair and ruin. As sinful humans, this happens—it's life here on earth. Yet God also grants us those extraordinary friends, who for whatever reason stick close by, ready to pick up part of the load that threatens to bury us.

In Christ, however, we find a truer friend than any other. For not only will Christ be in jail with you, but He will be in the same cell. Yet He did not and does not deserve jail time. He voluntarily entered the cell with us and took our place. We played, we partied, we passed the blame—and Christ took the blame. He won't leave us; His friendship will never lessen.

He loved us so greatly He bound Himself to us that we might be saved when the power of death came to call for us. Death called, but Christ answered. Death lost its power. "'Death has been swallowed up in victory. Where, O death, is your victory? Where, O death, is your sting?' The sting of death is sin, and the power of sin is the law.

But thanks be to God! He gives us the victory through our Lord Jesus Christ" (1 Corinthians 15:54b–57).

Now, through the power of Baptism and in the Holy Supper, we have been bound in Christ's death so that in Christ's life we might also be bound. Christ gave us freedom to live according to His calling. Instead of being bound in the prison of death, Christ freed us to share this wonderful message of glory with others. We are witness to this freedom in our words and our actions. We witness by living for Christ, a life known as the life of a sanctified sinner: "And He died for all, that those who live should no longer live for themselves but for Him who died for them and was raised again" (2 Corinthians 5:15).

With Christ, we can live to serve others. Building friendships that last because they are founded in our love for Christ. Caring, kindness and compassion accentuate and strengthen our interactions with those around us, granting us the opportunity to bear the load for someone else that they might see Christ in us.

> Gracious Father, friend of the friendless, grant that because of Your unending love for sinful humanity, we might seek out the friendless and forsaken that they might see you in all our actions, through Jesus Christ our Lord. Amen.

REMINISCENCE

Be imitators of God, therefore, as dearly loved children and live a life of love, just as Christ loved us and gave Himself up for us as a fragrant offering and sacrifice to God. Ephesians 5:1–2

LOVE WITH CHRIST

*Read: Deuteronomy 22:9–11;
2 Corinthians 6:14–18; and 1 John 4:7–12*

I started dating a girl the end of my senior year of high school. At that time I thought she was possibly "the one." We spent so much time together doing the things most normal teenagers do on dates, each of us believing we would be together forever.

However, something was missing in our relationship. My girlfriend had been baptized, but had only been to church a half dozen times in her life, mostly for weddings and baptisms. She did not really know much about Christ and His great love for us or what faith was. She did not know God, and was very set on not bringing Him into our relationship.

As a Christian, this placed great strain on me. Getting my girlfriend to come to church with me often meant that I had to bribe her into coming to worship and church activities. I would buy her gifts or get something for her to make her happy. It seemed like a worthwhile sacrifice since she was now going to church and maybe was opening herself to the Scriptures and the love of God. Gifts were not the answer though. Her heart was not open to Christ, and every opportunity I took to talk to her about my faith was met with indifference and a closed mind and heart.

Deuteronomy 22:10 discusses the yoking of an ox and a donkey. God tells the children of Israel not to do this. Wow, "off track" you are thinking. Yoking has everything to do with marriage. Not in the sense of "the ball and chain," but in the sense that the step and pace of a donkey and an ox are not the same. It does not plow the field well. In the same way, believers and unbelievers don't make good marriage partners. Paul reiterates God's warning in Corinthians.

A relationship without Christ as the center is difficult. As young adults many temptations come into a relationship. Overcoming these urges and temptations can be done with the strength only Christ can give. Not only does belief affect temptations, but also the direction of one's life. Most important though, a Christ-centered relationship can last because it is Christian love. We receive love from Christ and out of that we are able to selflessly love others. Christian love in a relationship is strong love. Worldly love is weak.

True love is a gift from God. It was displayed when He created human life in a perfect world, demonstrated again when He gave His only Son to die for us (1 John 4:9) and is seen everyday in our lives as we build relationships both with family and others, even in dating situations. Put God and His love into your relationships with people, His love will strengthen the love in your relationship and can make it lasting.

Find someone with whom you feel comfortable talking about Christ, someone who, along with you, will share your faith in Christ. The relationship will grow and be strong with the help of God! Remember love and relationships are a gift from God.

Heavenly Father, thank You for the gift of relationships. Help me to always place Christ at the center of the relationships I have. Let them grow with Your love as the center, and help me always to remember that relationships and the love shared between people are something You designed. Bless all the relationships in my life, in the name of Your Son, our Savior, Jesus Christ. Amen.

WAITING FOR LOVE

Read: Song of Songs 2:7

Ever wonder or worry, "God, am I going to be single for the rest of my life?" I remember going through high school and the beginning of college and seeing one by one my friends find boyfriends and girlfriends. Yet here I was 6 years and counting, still single, and still had not been on more then two dates in that entire span. I felt so alone at times because I wanted to be in a relationship so much. I worried constantly that something was wrong with me. What was I doing wrong? Did I smell funny? Talk weird?

For a long time I struggled in my faith, wondering if God was testing me by making me sacrifice something that I truly desired to prove my faith in Him. God wasn't doing that though; He wasn't trying to make me unhappy and wasn't expecting me to prove anything. Although I am still single, I have grown to see the amazing blessings God has given me. My worrying was for nothing as I see how God works only for our benefit.

When we are single, God allows us to grow to be our own unique individual person. This trust in Him has brought me even closer to Him. I have grown to rely on God first and foremost, not myself or someone else. Song of Songs 2:7 reminds us of this biblical promise. King Solomon is reminding the people of Jerusalem, and us, not to go looking for love. When we seek love for ourselves, we are not trusting in God or His plans. When we desperately search for love, we blind ourselves to traits or future problems that may arise. When we go looking for love, we fail to trust the one love that is always true, constant, and perfect—Christ's love for us. A love proved through sacrifice.

I encourage you to take Solomon's charge to heart. It won't be easy. There are always days when we will worry, be sad, and fail to trust God, but God's love will still be there waiting for us. We are never alone when we look to God to be first and foremost the love of our life. God, our God of omnipotent power and everlasting love, has a plan for you and me.

Dear Lord, You truly are a loving God and You alone are able to show and give perfect love. Your love looks beyond my human sinfulness through the death of Your Son, Jesus Christ. I thank You, Lord, for always loving me even when I fail to recognize it. I ask, Lord, that You give me strength and patience as I trust in Your plan for my life. In Jesus' name. Amen.

TO BE LOVED

Read: 1 John 4:7–10

On February 27, 2003, the world learned about the passing of Fred Rogers. Most adults who grew up on public television in the seventies and eighties probably remember the gentle, peaceful demeanor of Mr. Rogers. I loved watching him put on his cardigan and change his shoes, just as I loved the trolley trips into Make-Believe Land.

I would never imagine that I would be reflecting on him as I prepare to enter my final year in college. However, as an adult, looking back at that show, I realize now that the most important message I heard from Mister Rogers was that all people have the capacity to be loved and to love others.

During a tribute on a morning news show following Rogers' death, I saw a clip of Mr. Rogers giving a commencement address. In the address, he said, "You never have to do anything sensational to be loved."

These words struck me. This world searches for love in all of the wrong places. I see it all the time at my college. People strive to fit in to social groups and go to great lengths to get others to love them, but they are all misguided. Reflecting on Rogers' words led me to the ultimate source of love: God's gift of salvation. We *don't* have to do anything to be loved by God. In fact, we *can't* do anything good enough for God to love us. The plan of salvation and God's love for us seems foolish to the world because, as the saying goes, "Nothing in life is free."

We can rejoice that this is not the case with God. God's plan of salvation, thankfully, does not conform to the standards of the world. Despite our failures and shortcomings, God loved us enough to send His only Son, Jesus, to be our sacrifice, our replacement. In 1 John 4:10 Scripture says, "This is love: not that we loved God, but that He loved us and sent His Son as an atoning sacrifice for our sins."

Perfect love comes only through this realization that God is the fount, the ultimate source of love. We do not love others under our own power, but the love we have for others comes from God. God is love. In gratitude for the unconditional love shown to us through Jesus' sacrifice, we can show love to others.

> Dear heavenly Father, thank You for showing me what perfect love is. I praise and thank You that Your love for me does not depend on anything I do, but was made possible through the sacrificial death of Jesus Christ. Help me to be mindful of this sacrifice and live my life as a redeemed person. Help me to show Your love to others. In Jesus' name. Amen.

SAPPY LOVE

Read: Romans 13:8

Some days, the world looks just plain bleak. Oh, sure, the sun might be shining and birds chirping and dogs playing, but the storm clouds roll in as soon as you think of that one word—*love*. Forget that! Who wants to be a part of that whole business, holding hands and spending time together and smiling? Not you, that's for sure. You're just fine saving the word "love" for your grandparents and cookie dough ice cream, thank you very much.

Our culture is saturated with love today. From movies to television to music to your school, you can't take two steps without bumping into somebody who's "in love." And if you're the kind of person who isn't "in love", well, you might as well have a big scarlet "L" on your forehead for "loser." You know you aren't one, but being alone on a Friday night sure can give you doubts. If only you could find that "special someone." Maybe you have found them already. In that case, if only that "special someone" would just give you a chance. Then you could love them, and they'd love you, and you'd get married, and you'd have kids, and you'd live happily ever after.

In the book of Romans, St. Paul said that we owe love to one another. "Um, hello? St. Paul? I'm ready to owe all the love I've got, but nobody gives me a chance!" If St. Paul could respond to you, he would say, "I'm not talking about that kind of love." The kind of love Paul talked about runs much deeper than that. It's *agape*. You may have heard this word before; it is a selfless, all-encompassing love.

Whether or not you are dating someone, there is someone for you to love; in fact, there is a whole world out there for you to love. More important than that, there is someone who loves you, regardless of your status as single or happily taken—Jesus Christ. St. Paul wrote earlier in his epistle, "But God demonstrates His own love for us in this: While we were still sinners, Christ died for us" (Romans 5:8). In the midst of our sin and selfishness and unattractiveness, Jesus entered into the world, walked among us, and bore all our wrongs. He is "the one who loves another," fulfilling the Law. God loved us that much in that way.

Realistically, you may or may not find that "special someone." That's something you'll discover as you walk along the path of your life. Meanwhile, you have a commission from God Himself to love. Everyone you meet can be a "special someone" for you: not romantically, but in a reflection of Jesus' love. Even if you never find romantic love, eternal spiritual love has already found you in Baptism. And that is a love that will last for all time.

Lord God, You gave us Your Son, Jesus Christ, who is love itself, to die for us. Fill us with this love today and every day so we may proclaim Your Gospel to all people and praise Your holy name, through the same Jesus Christ our Lord. Amen.

His THOUGHTS

Read: Isaiah 55:8–9

Sometimes the dreams God has for us are bigger than the ones we have for ourselves. I have found this to be true many times in my life, especially when I look back at where I've been. Some things are just easier to see when you look back than when you look forward. It is in retrospect that we see the wisdom of God. We see how He grows us through our life experiences. The look back on our lives is a lesson in trust.

While in high school I wasn't very active socially. I typically found someone to eat lunch with, but didn't participate in many things after school. I was also an honors student, but lacked confidence in my abilities. I admit it. I was never a social butterfly. It was this way in high school and I anticipated it would continue in college. I lacked confidence in my abilities. The Lord had a plan to grow them when I went to college. My freshman year, my confidence in my abilities as a student grew as I became a TA. And socially I grew as I made friends and even joined a Christian fraternity.

God also taught me a lot about love. That first year, I broke up with my first boyfriend. I still wanted to get married, so I began dating a senior who I knew was looking for a wife. Within just a few months we were engaged.

There were so many things wrong with our relationship, but I was unwilling to admit it. So I kept pushing off the wedding date. Finally I was forced to face facts one evening. My fiancé had graduated by that point, and wasn't there when the conversation turned to why people get married. I listened to most of it, but when I was asked why I was getting married, I realized that I didn't have an answer. I broke off my engagement the next day.

I realized that I had been directing my life, not God. I wanted to get married so badly that the guy wasn't important, nor was love. We often lie to ourselves, telling ourselves we are in control of our lives, that we know what we want and that we know what is best. But God can tear down our pride, humbling us. And when we are broken, He shows us the door where we were trying to fit through a window.

Isaiah discusses the difference between God's thoughts and ours. God has a plan for each of us, a plan for our lives. A plan for joy and peace (verse 12). God will never leave us, He promised us that. He will also lead us, another of His promises. Although we may never see it, His leading has a purpose and a blessing.

Yeah, for a while my life was lonely, but God provided for that. With His strength and with the gift of friends, I survived and am better for it. I could have fallen into the trap of wondering why this all happened. But I know God has in store for me peace and joy, great plans I would have otherwise limited. Thanks be to Him, that unlike us, God allows limitless skies.

Dear Lord, I am coming to a new time in my life where I will learn new things about myself and about You. Please help me to listen to Your guidance, and to know that although I am limited, You are limitless, and Your grace is sufficient for me. In Your name I pray. Amen.

PERFECT LOVE

Read: Ephesians 3:17–19

So, here it is again, another February 14th. I gotta tell ya—I'm 23 years old and I haven't had a Valentine's Day yet that I didn't hate. Until now, that is. I used to struggle on this day because I didn't have someone to tell me they love me. And I didn't have someone to call when I got home to say "I love you." And then it hit me. I have someone who loves me more than I will ever understand.

John 15:13 tells us how loved we are in the words, "Greater love has no one than this, that he lay down his life for his friends." I finally took a minute to think again about what that means. The almighty God, master of the universe, *loves* me. He loves *me* so much that He gave His life up. It wasn't the nails that held Him on the cross; it was His love for me—and for you. He calls us friends and loves us with perfect love. Perfect love! Can you imagine?

February 14th. Well, here's how it is: some people have found the person they want to share the rest of their lives with. Others have given their heart to someone and not received the same in return. And still others go through each day trusting in the faithfulness of God, waiting. . . .

Wherever you're at in life, I pray that today you may be overwhelmed by the love our Savior has for you. I pray that you are consumed by its vastness and in awe of its power. And today, may it reign peace in your heart like you've never known before.

On February 14th, like any other day, God shows His love for us in His Son and on the cross. May you know today and always the depth and breadth of Christ's love for you.

Lord Jesus, thank You for this day that allows us to think about love. Your love is amazing and we're so grateful. Surround us in that love today. Fill us with Your Spirit so we may catch a glimpse of Your perfect love. Thank You for loving us more than we'll ever understand. In Jesus' Name. Amen.

TRUST ME

Read: Proverbs 3:5–6

Many things happen in this world that do not seem to make sense and we often find ourselves asking God, "Why?" Why does it seem that just as you start to put the final piece in place, the puzzle falls apart and the pieces scatter everywhere?

I recently watched my puzzle break into a thousand bits and my heart went with it. Charlie and I had always been a couple. He was not only my boyfriend, but also my friend. We spent every moment we could together. Everything about him seemed right, but with just six little words my clear-cut picture of life was thrown out of whack! "I want to see other people." I would hear those words play in my head over and over again, making me feel worthless and confused. Why? I just did not understand.

I tried to preoccupy myself with other things, hoping to keep my mind off of him. I put much effort into making new friends and hanging with my best friend. I also spent my time talking to God for strength. My mom has a very strong faith and she helped remind me to talk to God in prayer, claiming it would help when I was down.

Eventually, I started to understand why it all happened. God drew me closer to Him and my family. It made me aware of the separation between my best friend and myself, and helped save our friendship. I learned so much about relationships that I can apply to the future. I would never change what happened because I definitely gained more than I lost.

Sometimes it's very hard to see the reasons behind the pain and suffering we endure, but God has a plan for us. We can trust God that He knows what's best and that He has something better in store for us.

Dear heavenly Father, Your plan is greater than any I can comprehend. Consequently, at times it is hard for me to see why things happen the way they do. Help remind me that after every low there is a better time to come. Take my hand and guide me Lord, and when I can walk no more, carry me in Your loving arms. In Jesus' name. Amen.

There is a time for everything,
and a season for every activity
under heaven. Ecclesiastes 3:1

REVIEW

COFFEE DEPENDENCY

Read: Romans 12:1–3

Before I came to college, I had not encountered the world of coffee. Café mochas, lattes, frappuccinos, or cappuccinos—they were all foreign to me, but I soon learned how important they would become to me. Sipping a cup of strong coffee in the campus coffee shop was the "in" thing to do. Coeds "studiously" surveying books with a $3.95 latte in one hand looked like a scene right out of a commercial. I began to understand, though, that coffee was important for far more than just the college atmosphere. Coffee was important to stay awake! There were many nights when I slipped over to the coffee shop or brewed up a pot of strong coffee to keep going through the mounds of term papers and projects. Finals time always seemed to induce the sight of weary young college students stumbling into class clutching that final project, and, you guessed it, a mug of coffee.

It's strange and a little disheartening to think of how dependent we are on things to make us feel better. Coffee seemed to do the trick. Using coffee to become a part of a group and to keep me going through the late nights was foolish. Sometimes I got frustrated when the caffeine buzz would wear off and my work was yet to be completed. We get frustrated because we have tried to control our own lives but we are not successful. In Proverbs 3:5–6, we are reminded that we don't have to rely on ourselves. When we put our full trust in the Lord instead of using foolish methods like coffee to get us through the day we are successful.

Now, I do not mean to say that you should rely on God's divine inspiration until the night before your paper or project is due. It may be helpful to brainstorm that one a few weeks before hand. At the same time don't plan on the coffee to keep you up. It is more than coffee's caffeine that you depend on when you do this. When you plan on the coffee to get you through the all-nighter, you have put your trust in the substance, not the Lord. Your first thought in this is not God, but coffee.

When we feel fear or anxiety over things yet to be completed or deadlines to be met, we can trust fully in God's promises because only He will truly fulfill us. Jesus' death on the cross was the ultimate fulfillment of God's promise to us. When we put our trust in the crucified and risen Lord Jesus, we will never be put to shame and that buzz will never wear off!

So maybe you are feeling the pain of heavy eyelids and a headache when you look at your to do list. It's okay, you are a forgiven child of God. Yes, the projects and papers still need to be finished. Take with you the peace of the strength of Christ.

Lord, thank You that I don't have to rely on my foolish ways in this world. Help me to trust in You for every aspect of my life. I praise you that I am not alone in this world; You are there making my paths straight. In Jesus' name. Amen.

TIME TO REST

Read: Psalm 90 and Genesis 2:1–3

In your college orientation seminars you may hear the term "time management." In fact you may have a whole unit in a freshman seminar class devoted to the topic. In the years to come you'll definitely hear about it. In college, time management will mean studying first, then playing video games. Or planning your research paper four or five weeks before it is due (as opposed to picking the topic the night before). Time management means planning your day, so much time for each task, errand, job, and fun. There will never seem to be enough time to do everything. The result is to do lists, multi-tasking, daily planners, prioritization, fast food, caffeine, adrenaline, and constant quick fixes. Sadly, as you get older there will be more and more demands on your time. Life only gets busier. This is not to scare you; it's just reality.

Now imagine for a moment a world without time demands. There are no alarm clocks, calendars, bedtimes, New Year's Eve celebrations, or even deadlines. This is kind of how God exists. There are no time barriers or limits for Him. He never gets tired or needs to stop to take a rest. His brain never gets frazzled after pulling an all-nighter. He doesn't fear the passing of time and never ages. He is unchanging. He exists outside of time. It is an existence that is truly heavenly. He invites us to be with Him in that kind of existence after we die. And not only that, He provides us with a few glimpses of such a thing here through Holy Communion, the Bible, personal prayer time, and Sabbath rest.

Now, proper time management can be a useful thing that can help people to more effectively use the time God has gives them here on earth. But often forgotten or neglected in our organizational planner world is the idea of Sabbath rest. God created the universe in six days. He could have easily done it in less than that, and He was by no means tired, but on the seventh day He chose to rest to provide an example for us. It's even one of the 10 Commandments, "Remember the Sabbath day by keeping it holy" (Exodus 20:8). God emphasized this repeatedly because He knows us too well. He knows that when we get really busy, we sometimes lose focus on what's really important and start to concentrate too much on ourselves and our problems. And we start forgetting about God.

God went to great lengths to encourage and command us to take a Sabbath rest, not only for the renewal of our minds and bodies, but also our souls. He wants us to make time to be with Him, to grow in Him, and to allow the Spirit to work in us in new and exciting ways. Oftentimes we let our own business get in the way of our relationship with Him. But when we repent, our amazing God is continually merciful and is constantly longing for us to spend time with Him and His Word.

> Dear Lord, I am sorry for the times I have pushed You aside and put other priorities before You. Please give me the willingness to spend time with You every day. Thank You for providing me with a Sabbath rest not only every Sunday, but also for all eternity. In Jesus' name. Amen.

FREEDOM

Read: Deuteronomy 5:16

Welcome to college! Perhaps this is your first time away from home or maybe you're used to being away from your parents. Either way, you are probably thinking, "FREEDOM!!!!" "NO MORE PARENTS!!!"

When I moved to college, I felt on top of the world. "Freedom at last," or so I thought. No more parental rules. No more of dad saying, "as long as you're under my roof." No more curfews. No more forcing me to do my homework. No set bedtime. I didn't even have to eat if I didn't want to! I was at the beginning of my freshman year. I was at the start of the rest of my life! Oh, I wish I would have known better . . .

The first semester I was at school I didn't follow any of my household rules. Frequently, I stayed out until 3:00 A.M.—especially the nights before big exams. I wasn't forced to do homework, so I hardly did any at all. I didn't go to bed at a logical hour. I didn't wake up for early morning classes. Plain and simple, I abused my freedom.

My abuse of my freedom led to some severe consequences. I didn't have the grade point I really wanted. I didn't have the energy to participate in many of the activities I wanted to do. I just didn't have any purpose for being away at school.

The abuse of freedom is nothing new. First, Adam and Eve abused their freedom in the garden and rebelled against God by eating the forbidden fruit. Then, the children of Israel abused their freedom by worshipping the golden calf. David abused his freedom by sleeping with

Bathsheba. Today, we abuse our freedom by disobeying our parents. The consequence is huge for abusing freedom. Adam and Eve were cast out of the garden and all humanity was cursed. Israel wandered for 40 years. David had an illegitimate child. We experience hardship, fatigue, and other reactions to our abuse of freedom.

God gives us parents not only as guides, but as His representatives on this earth. The rules we grow up with help us to live Christ-like lives as we grow older. In Deuteronomy, God attaches the promise of long life and good living to those who honor or respect their parents. This promise is rooted in freedom. Parents raise children to live their lives for Christ. As we mature, we are given the freedom by our parents to live our own lives; however, we often abuse it. The promise is then terminated. We are doomed. Our freedom is destroyed.

But thanks be to God for His promise of Christ Jesus and for Him setting us free once again! Free from sin. True freedom! This is the promise of eternal life and godly living to those who believe. Although we abuse our earthly freedom time and time again, we rest in the promise that we are forgiven. We abuse His commands and we abuse His freedom. But thanks be to Jesus for giving us the freedom of heaven and lasting comfort in Him.

> Almighty God, thank You for the freedom that You give us. Although we destroy that freedom, You constantly renew it through Your Son, Jesus. Let us live in that freedom that You give. Empower us to make responsible choices that glorify You in everything. In Jesus' name we pray. Amen.

GETTING FED FROM THE VINE

Read: John 15:1–16

"Fed from the Vine," sounds like a great college course in wine tasting or an excuse to drink something outside of the keg. For many, college is like *Animal House*, a continual barrage of kegs and parties. But what fruit does this bear? A night apart from the day's trouble, fun, sickness, a pounding headache?

John warns us of the fruit we bear in John 15. We are to bear good fruit. John mentions the fruit of love. We are to show love to our neighbor. This is not only in our kindness and our actions, but in sharing true love with them—sharing the message of Christ!

Graduating from high school can be an empowering experience. When one has received his or her well-deserved diploma, college scholarships, and other honors, it can be easy to develop a mindset of self-sufficiency. One may even say, "Now that I've made it through high school, I am free to go off to college and do whatever I want to. I can take care of myself." While this may be true in some circumstances, it is the farthest thing from the truth in spiritual matters. If high school wasn't bad enough, college provides many new opportunities for God's children to fall prey to the world. Whether it is pre-marital sex, drinking parties, drug experiments, or crude joking, Satan is going to continue to use the self-sufficient mindset to lead Christian college students in directions they would really rather not go. Jesus once again offers us great comfort for these special years of our lives.

In John 15, He tells us He is the Vine that we live off of.

Just as a plant has a main vine or trunk with many branches growing from it, so also Jesus provides the spiritual food that we need to continue to grow in our faith as Christians. Through the hearing of His Word, the precious waters of Baptism, and the real presence of His body and blood in Communion, He truly is our provider for all areas of our lives. He even prays for us! He says in John 17:9, "I pray for them. I am not praying for the world, but for those You have given me, for they are Yours." What a loving and powerful God we have! He died for our sins, prays for us, and continues to provide us with all we need to survive whatever comes our way in this life—even college!

So while you are at college, take pride in your past accomplishments but realize that God has even greater things in store for you. Resist the world's temptations with God's power, remembering that if you remain in Jesus Christ, He will remain in you and cause you to produce much fruit for His kingdom. Apart from Jesus, we truly can do nothing. But thanks to God, the Gardener, who sent His Son to be our Vine and our Savior at the cross of Calvary!

> Precious Vine, I thank You for transforming my life every new day. By Your power, guide my decision making that it may always show to those around me that I belong to You and am proud to bear the name of Jesus Christ. I give thanks to You for suffering in my place at Calvary. Although I do not deserve it, I am honored that You have called me to be Your "branch." Amen.

SPIRITUAL FOOD

Read: John 6:48–58

Living away from home will make you appreciate many things. One thing you are sure to appreciate is your mom's home cooking. At times the cafeteria fare will appear inedible. Before too long you may memorize the Domino's number. They might even know you by name. Whether it is your mom's best home-cooked dinner or your favorite meal at a restaurant, we all look forward to eating. Food is an essential and enjoyable part of our lives. It is also a necessity. Food gives us strength and energy to live and work. For some, food also is a source of comfort. Any girl after a break-up can tell you the power of chocolate or ice cream.

In John 6, Jesus tells us the importance of another kind of food—spiritual food. Is this section of Scripture Jesus explains the importance of Holy Communion. Eternal life and forgiveness await us in this meal. Communion is not the only spiritual food we may receive. God's Word also feeds us with God's promises. How comforting to know that God is with us, forgiving us and loving us.

If we understand how important food is in our lives, then why do we have such a hard time with being spiritually fed? Many people lose sight of the importance of worship, Christian fellowship, and the Word because they lose sight of the gifts God brings to us in these means. Can you imagine if these people thought the same way about food? What if a person decided there was no merit in eating. They would lose their strength, become weak, and eventually die.

We know we need food to live. The same thing is true of spiritual food. In God's Word, our faith is kept alive. Christ's love, forgiveness, and grace is what saves our dying souls. As Jesus says in John 6:51, "I am the living bread that came down from heaven. If anyone eats of this bread, he will live forever. This bread is my flesh, which I will give for the life of the world." Jesus came down from heaven and lived a perfect life, but He gave His life by dying on the cross for the sins of the entire world. He did it out of His great love for us so we can spend eternity in heaven with Him.

God gave us such an incredible gift through His Son that we not only need God's Word, but we *want* to keep hearing those promises. It gives us strength and energy for the day. It comforts and soothes our souls. It reminds us that no matter what happens in our lives nothing can ever separate us from God's love which Christ Jesus our Lord shows us (Romans 8:38–39). Remember the most important thing in our lives is Jesus, the Bread of Life, who gives us eternal life. When you're planning your dinners out this week, plan one with Him.

> Thank You Jesus for loving me, dying for me, and giving me the gift of heaven. Thank You for feeding me with Your Word. May I remember Your promises and all of the blessings you give me each and everyday. In Your holy name I pray. Amen.

A SHOT OF THE HOLY SPIRIT

Read: Ephesians 5:15–18

College! Finally I was getting out of the house and getting out on my own!

Learning, in college, takes place both in and out of the classroom. I figured that with the sheltered life I had led for the past 18 years, I had a lot to learn. My knowledge of alcohol was limited to TV commercials and college stories. However, everyone around me seemed to know how to drink, what was good, and what was bad. For the first month or two I was able to come up with excuses for not going out to drink and party, but my reasons eventually started sounding weak. Finally I gave in and went out. That night I stumbled home feeling something I had never felt before. Everything seemed funny and I felt like I had the courage of ten men. I had learned a new way of life. But this learning came with a headache.

The next couple of weekends I went out with friends, each time partaking in more kinds of drinks. Finally, one night I watched a team of paramedics take a friend of mine out on a stretcher. I decided that going out every weekend and getting drunk wasn't the life I should be leading. I realized that in my partying I had pushed God out of my life. It wasn't that I didn't need Him, it was the fact that I felt guilty for my actions every time I thought of Him.

That night after the ambulance left, one of the guys on my floor, who I didn't know well, invited me to a

Saturday night worship service. I went with him the next weekend and the pastor was talking about the temptations of alcohol. He quoted Ephesians 5:18 and I remembered that having the Holy Spirit in me was better than any kind of frosty beverage. The Spirit didn't leave me feeling empty the next day and certainly didn't cause any headaches. Being filled with the Spirit rather than alcohol allowed me to feel the grace and love of God rather than the false courage and guilt that alcohol had granted me.

As I became more involved in church, I realized that college is not all about partying and getting drunk. Many people don't drink and don't go to the bars. There are so many better things to do at school than drink. Fill yourself with the Holy Spirit! It's the best thing to fill up on when living on your own.

> Heavenly Father, being out on my own can be difficult. The world has so many temptations and drinking is one of them. Help me to fill myself not with alcohol but with your intoxicating love and the Holy Spirit! In Jesus' name. Amen.

FRIENDS MAY FAIL

Read: Job 19:19; Hebrews 13:5b

"What happened to all my friends?" I often wondered that summer. The group of girls I seemed to have spent the majority of my high school years with practically vanished. They were all still there, just distanced. These were the girls I went to every dance with, shared secrets and problems with; and then it was as if we were no more than acquaintances.

We had all graduated in June, with the whole summer ahead of us. Plans of road trips, graduation parties, and college preparations stretched as far as the eye could see. However, a few weeks into the summer, it was quite clear that none of these friends was going to make an effort to stay in touch. They started to hang out with another group who did not have a very good influence on them. Before I knew it, my friends were getting drunk and engaging in other dangerous activities almost every single night. They had really changed.

Although I knew what they were doing, I was still hurt to not be invited. I felt betrayed and frustrated. I did, however, find a little hope that maybe they didn't invite me because they knew I'd say no. Maybe my convictions had rubbed off a little.

That summer helped me figure out who my real friends were. I went on a few church trips, got back in touch with some old friends and even started a little support group with some close friends from church.

I grew in my faith that summer. God is a friend who

will stick closer than a brother. I know friends are not perfect, and we will all make mistakes. But I know He will be there even as everyone else fails. Through the Holy Spirit, I learned to put my faith and trust in Jesus. Jesus gives us forgiveness for our sin and calls us to live a life guided by His Word. Even when I—or my friends—wander from His path and make mistakes, He will not leave or forsake me. He will be my friend through all of my ups and downs, the friend-filled and the friendless times.

> Dear Lord, please help me to find the friends who are true. Help me to be a good friend and an example to others. Please bless all my friends and keep them in Your arms. In Jesus' name. Amen.

WHEN THINGS GO WRONG

Read: Colossians 1:24

Feeling like life on your own is hard? Feeling like it is tough being your own boss, when to wake or sleep, who to hang out with, what party to attend? Temptation seems to be lurking behind every door. You are meeting new people and able to have new experiences. Sometimes the cause seems clear, a clear right and a clear wrong; other times the line seems blurred. No doubt about it—life is hard!

If anyone knew hardship, it was the Apostle Paul. Having been nearly stoned to death, jailed, shipwrecked, and more, he was no stranger to tough times. Now, if all these things happen to you in your first week at college, perhaps you should consider transferring (just kidding). Paul's words in Colossians 1:24 provide great comfort to those who bear the name of Jesus Christ and are undergoing tough times because of it.

College is a time when one's faith can easily be challenged. With all the pressure to experiment with sex, drugs, alcohol, and new religions, a Christian college student can expect to be often left out and to feel alone. Paul went through these same trials. In fact, he described his intense struggles as a participation in the suffering of Jesus Christ. Paul is not saying that Christ's death on the cross was not sufficient for our salvation. Rather, he refers to the persecution that those who bear the name of Jesus will face. Here is where the comfort of the "Theology of the Cross" comes in. Nowhere in Scripture did Jesus promise that the Christian life would be full of health, wealth, and relaxation. He Himself was proof of this. The slandering, beating, and tears of Good Friday were the culmination of the sins of the world being placed on the very shoulders of the Son of God. Trials that come our way in college and in our entire lives are just a drop in the bucket compared to what Jesus suffered for us. Thanks be to God that Christ conquered sin, death, and hell at Calvary.

Like the apostle Paul, we know the trials of the Christian life mean taking up *our* crosses and following Jesus. The comfort in this hardship is that Christ will never allow anything to come our way that is more than we can handle by the power He gives us, and He will always provide a way out. May He continue to strengthen us by the power of His Word and Sacraments when we face trials and suffering for His name.

> Lord Jesus, please help me to be always grateful to You for the cross. You are my God and my Savior; I trust You fully to guide me throughout the days of my life. In times of suffering, comfort me and let me know You are always at my side. I am eternally grateful for the suffering You endured for me, a sinner. Thank You for this special time in my life. May I serve You always, as Your Spirit works in me. Amen.

RECALL

But God has surely listened and heard my voice in prayer.
Praise be to God, who has not rejected my prayer
or withheld His love from me. Psalm 66:19–20

I AM WITH YOU ALWAYS

Read: Mathew 28:20, Psalm 63

Leaving home to spread your wings and fly is never an easy task. It means leaving behind the cushion and comfort of your home, going out and learning to support yourself.

I remember my transition from my parents' home to college life. The drive from home to the dorms was only an hour long, but it was very significant. That hour was filled with excitement and trepidation. Within that hour I was getting farther from close friends, people who loved me, and people whom I knew and trusted. As I got closer to school, I was getting nearer to strangers and to the unknown.

As my parents left me in my cold, uninviting dorm room, I remember clinging to my mother in a hug, desperately desiring to go back with them. Perhaps it was all just a joke; in a week's time I would be back home, just like when I left home for camp.

It wasn't a joke. I was in college, embarking on a whole new life full of possibilities. The transition was a very hard time for me, with tons of phone calls home and many weekend visits. Gradually these decreased as I began developing a life of my own, depending more on God for my support instead of on my parents.

The funny thing is: never once did I feel utterly lonely. Even as I sat alone in my dorm room the first night, bare walls and all, I didn't feel alone. As a Christian, I knew a wonderful friendship with our Lord and Savior,

Jesus Christ, who promised to be with me always. Knowing I have a God always there supporting me, providing for my needs, and upholding me is a tremendous consolation. Those times when I just need an ear to listen, and no one was even a phone call away, God was there. When there was something heavy on my heart and I didn't want to share it with new or old friends or family, Jesus was there to listen and give comfort. What a comfort it is to have a direct line to God through prayer. God desires us to talk to Him and tell Him what is going on in our lives. He always offers a listening ear.

As I learned to deal with feelings of homesickness, I learned to share them with God and ask for His strength. God strengthened me, and as He did my prayers moved from focusing on myself and my problems to encompass others.

In those times when we feel most lonely, it is easy to drown in sadness and despair (we've all gotten caught in the trap). Yet when we turn our focus to God and what He has done for us, we have the peace that only He can give.

> Heavenly Father, thank You so much for listening to me, loving me, and supporting me. I pray that You would help me to depend on You in all things. Grant me the peace, which only You can give. In Jesus' name. Amen.

I WANT WHAT YOU'RE HAVING

Read: 1 John 5:19 and John 3:16–21

I wish someone had told me what to really expect from college roommates. I had heard stories about quirky and eccentric roommates and even downright mean roommates, but I had sadly not heard much about witnessing to a roommate.

I never understood why I ended up with Dana. She and I had absolutely nothing in common, yet we always ended up in the same places. She struggled with religion. During her first two years in college she had run the gamut of religions, from Christianity to paganism. When I moved into an apartment, we ended up being roommates. We got along okay, but the tension of religion was always at the forefront. My other roommate, Susan, and I always made an effort to invite Dana to our Bible study and to church, but she politely refused. We prayed for Dana, asking God to break down the walls she had built around her heart. One night, Dana called us all together and lectured us on how much she was offended and confused by our faith. She said all we talked about was church and Bible study. She was tired of us inviting her to religious functions. She told us she felt uncomfortable.

I was embarrassed because I knew I did not always live a life that reflected my faith, although she claimed I did. I was shocked that our witnessing had seemingly backfired. We seemed to be driving her off. I was scared as I searched for the right words to share with Dana. I told Dana that Susan and I shared our faith with her because Christianity is a religion of love. We share the message of Christ's salvation because His death is the ultimate testament of love.

God's Word is powerful; as I sat there looking at my roommate, I knew that Dana just needed to be loved.

"Dana, I love you; Susan loves you; and most of all, God loves you. And that isn't going to change."

Tears began streaming down Dana's face as she told us about how anguished she felt about religion. "I just want what you guys have," Dana said.

"It's called joy, Dana. We have joy because we have Jesus, and you can have Him, too," I said.

Dana wasn't falling away. God was pulling her closer. Her uncomfortable feelings were the crumbling walls we had prayed for. The seed has been planted in Dana's heart, and I pray that the Holy Spirit continues to work on her and sends people to share the joyful message of salvation with her.

Witnessing is scary. It puts us on the line to defend *whose* we are. But it is not as intimidating as knowing what is ahead of those who do not know our Savior. It turns that back-burner message into a burning fire. Often times we worry about how to spread that message. We go to great lengths to develop ways to do so. I learned that sharing Christ can come in the small way of invitations and friendship.

> Lord, thank You for the joy of Jesus. Help us to reach out to lost souls like Dana and to be bold for You. Your Word is powerful. May we use it to bring light to the darkest depths. In Jesus' name. Amen.

Wake Up!!!

Read: 1 Thessalonians 5:1–11

During the first week of college, the event I remember most was the first fire drill. I didn't want to believe that the residence hall directors would be so cruel as to plan a fire alarm at 5:30 A.M., but I was wrong. I remember hearing the piercing noise of the alarm and seeing the strobe lights flashing outside of my window. I jumped out of my bed and rushed to wake my roommate, whom I had only known for about twelve hours. I slipped into my neon green shower shoes, pulled on my purple robe, and headed for the lobby. I remember standing out on the lawn with 500 other sleep deprived females who looked as equally disoriented and ridiculous in their pajamas as I. Although we had only been at college for one day, we were learning about being prepared for the inevitable.

While I didn't think that 5:30 A.M. was a good time for a fire drill, I realized that being prepared is essential. That's the way our faith walk is. It's about preparing and daily going to God's Word to prepare ourselves to deal with all aspects of life. God's Word helps us to prepare for the times of joy and happiness, like a wedding, a birth, a promotion, or hanging out with friends. But it also prepares us to deal with the times of trial, such as a death, the loss of a job, or an illness. God's Word provides a guide for our lives to show us the way to go. We don't have the answers in ourselves, but we know where to find them.

Paul wrote to the Thessalonians to encourage them in the midst of their persecution. He wrote to give hope and comfort to those who were suffering for bearing the name Christian. He also wrote to them to be prepared not only to stand for what they believe, but also to remain faithful to God and not fall back into the paganism they were raised in.

God's Word speaks not only to people thousands of years ago, but to us today. He writes to us with that same message: I have bought heaven for you. It is coming, be prepared. Remain faithful to Me. I love you and will give you the strength you need.

Meditation on God's Word and the preparation of our hearts is planning that cannot be underestimated. We don't know when Christ will return to take us home. Like an unexpected fire, it could come at any time. But when we rely on God's Word and study His Scriptures diligently, we have God sharing Himself and His message with us. Like a fire drill that makes sleep deprived students aware of the procedure and assured of their safety, God's Word assures us of His guidance and strength. We are forgiven children relying on a Savior who is preparing a place for us.

> Dear Lord, thank You for the promises You give me in Your Word. Send Your Holy Spirit to me to keep me faithful as I study and reflect on Your promises. In Jesus' name. Amen.

VOICE OF GOD

Read: Proverbs 2:1–15

How often have you prayed and waited for an answer? Many times I pray for days and still never seem to get an answer. I often wonder if I'm just looking too deep into what God is trying to tell me. Sometimes it can be right in front of my eyes, but I spend too much time looking into the details, making it hard to see the actual picture being given.

One night four years ago I decided to pray for God to lead me in the right direction, help me with school, and help me focus on important things in life. I said my prayer not expecting an answer. Then I flipped open my Bible and read Proverbs 2:9–15:

> Then you will understand what is right and just and fair—every good path. For wisdom will enter your heart and knowledge will be pleasant to your soul. Discretion will protect you, and understanding will guard you. Wisdom will save you from the ways of wicked men, from men whose words are perverse, who leave the straight paths to walk in dark ways who delight in doing wrong and rejoice in the perverseness of evil, whose paths are crooked and who are devious in their ways.

My mind was blown. Everything I'd prayed about was summed up in these verses. Ever since that moment, when I pray, I don't pray for quick answers. I know God has an answer and in His time He will make it known to me. Christ is my Good Shepherd and guides me on His path of righteousness.

Is it possible that God will respond to us in such simple situations through prayer and that the answers to life's problems are no further than our very own Bible? Yes! As Romans 12:12 reminds us, "Be joyful in hope, patient in affliction, faithful in prayer."

Dear Lord: Open my ears, my eyes, and my mind to the words You so clearly send to me through Your written Word. Help me lift up my troubles to You in prayer, knowing that You love me and will protect me. In Jesus' name. Amen.

THE UNAVOIDABLE

Read: 1 Thessalonians 4:13–18

Medicine, healthcare plans, seatbelts. As much as we try to avoid it—death is unavoidable. It is nearly impossible to turn on the news, a movie, or a song without some mention of it. It may even impact you on a personal level with the loss of a relative or friend. The scary part is that death doesn't take age into account. Youth doesn't protect you. You may know of people your age who have died from injury or disease. It's easy to feel invincible when you're a young adult, but seeing someone your age or younger in a casket quickly reminds you of your mortality.

When someone close to us dies, it's like a punch to the stomach. This person whom we loved and spent time with is gone, and it seems that we'll never see him or her again. St. Paul encourages us to think differently. As Christians, we know this life isn't all there is. The Christian has read the "whole story" and knows it ends with a "happily ever after." As St. Paul wrote, "We will be with the Lord forever" (1 Thessalonians 4:17b). There isn't a better ending in any novel or movie ever written.

It's natural for anybody, even believers in Christ, to get discouraged when somebody close to them dies. Even the early church in Thessalonica was uninformed and needed a reminder in this letter about the saints who had died. Paul reminded them and us that we "do not grieve like the rest of men, who have no hope" (1 Thessalonians 4:13b). Christians have this hope, which is the "hope of eternal life which God, who does not lie, promised before the beginning of time" (Titus 1:2). This hope is Jesus Christ. Those who are baptized and believe in Him need not fear death because death has been swallowed up in Christ's resurrection (Isaiah 25:8).

Death can terrify, that's for certain. It is the just wages for our sins. But Christ took the cross and paid that wage, giving us the free gift of eternal life in Him (Romans 6:23). Now, when we are confronted with death, we do not mourn forever, but rejoice in the hope of the resurrection and share that Good News with others.

Heavenly Father, You gave Your Son, Jesus Christ, to die on the cross that I might not have to face eternal death. I pray that You would send Your Holy Spirit to give me the hope of the resurrection. Through Jesus Christ our Lord. Amen.

ANSWERED @ JESUS.COM

Read: Matthew 6:8–14 and Psalm 6

I always thought it would be great if God operated through e-mail. My life would be less stressful if I could just shoot God a memo at my convenience and then check a few things off the old to do list. Turn over concerns about Grandma's health . . . check! Ask God for safe travel as I go home this weekend . . . check! Ask God for wisdom in budgeting my expenses so I can pay tuition next semester . . . check! To top it all off, if God had e-mail He could just reply back to my concerns.

Dear Heather,

Thanks for the memo about your concerns. I wanted to let you know that I love your grandmother and she is My child; I will take care of her. Don't worry about your trip home this weekend; My angels will be protecting you. I provide for the birds and the flowers and I will provide for all of your needs, too. Be sure to keep in touch!

Love, God

E-mail is great! You get instant communication all from the convenience of your personal computer! E-mail allows you to give only the information you want, no minutes spent chatting on the phone about meaningless stuff, no trying to figure out tone of voice or non-verbal clues about what the person means—just straight information. Life would be simpler if I could just go to my address book and know that God is only a click away.

Yet e-mails can be a source of frustration. Return messages saying the message was undeliverable because the e-mail address was wrong or the mailbox was full takes away from the convenience of the whole system. Then I wonder if I have to try again later, what do I do to send the message? Why won't the Internet fairies fly fast enough today to deliver my message?

Not knowing if your message was sent or why it didn't send or what to do about it can be frustrating. And if it is sent, I never know if the receiver actually understood what I was saying. Or if the person is who they say they are.

It is a good thing God gives us His communication systems to use and not our faulty ones. God gives us a very powerful means of communicating with Him—prayer. Prayer is available to us 24 hours a day, 7 days a week, and our messages never come back undeliverable. We are guaranteed that the concerns we give to God via this powerful faith medium are delivered directly to Him and answered by Him. Our all-knowing God hears our prayers—both those said aloud and those concerns that are on our heart.

The best part is God wants us to pray; God wants us to give Him our cares. He wants to bear our burdens for us. He wants to give us comfort. Prayer lightens our load and gives the load to God. He promises to answer every prayer according to His good and gracious will.

Thank You, God, for giving us the wonderful gift of prayer that we may share our concerns with You. We praise You that You willingly bear our burdens for us. Help us to always come to You, our only source of hope and salvation. In Christ's holy name I pray. Amen.

THEY JUST NEED JESUS

Read: Joshua 1:5

When I graduated from high school, I did not have a clue about the various paths that peoples' lives could take. In my graduation address to my classmates, I encouraged everyone to take the path less traveled. "Blaze a new trail," I ambitiously asserted. In our purple robes and caps, we all looked like we could be destined for the same thing—greatness. I moved to college and began my own life and the rest of my classmates went their own way. It seems that high school adequately prepared me to deal with the academic challenges, but I wish someone had prepared me for dealing with the lives of others.

While watching the 10:00 news one night, I saw that the husband of one of my high school classmates had been arrested for the heinous beating death of their three-month-old baby. My heart dropped. How do things like this happen? I came from the same town as this young mother. We played badminton in the same P.E. class in high school. We sat in the same classes and heard the same lessons. How was it that she ended up with two children by the age of twenty, working 50 hours a week at a gas station, married to a man who was suspected of murdering their child? Suddenly the term paper on my computer screen seemed unimportant.

Sin corrupts every area of human life. No one is immune to the pain and suffering sin causes. After I got over the initial anger, sadness filled my heart as I realized that this story is played out in too many homes across the country. Children are abused and people's lives take tragic turns. The news is filled with stories of pain and heartache. Life seems hopeless for many people, because the perfect world God created is corrupted by sin.

Yet the pain and hopelessness do not have to reign over our lives. God gave us a way out. Christ's sacrifice on the cross and His glorious resurrection eliminated eternal death for all who believe in Him. On the Last Day, He will come to take us home with Him forever.

The hope of Jesus Christ is a message that this dying world desperately needs to hear. Some are so wrapped up in evil and tragedy, they think it is the only way to live. As Christians who know the redeeming power of God's love, we can share with others the message of eternal life with Christ.

> Lord, grant me the courage to share Your message of salvation to a world dying without hope. Help me to recognize the opportunities to comfort and support others with Your Word. In Jesus' name. Amen.

CONVERSATION HELP

Read: Colossians 4:2

As a senior, there is probably no time more important to me as a college student than time spent praying. James tells us we have not because we ask not. Jesus says ask and it shall be given. Paul tells us to pray without ceasing. Now, these words must be read in context to be properly understood, but they make the point of the importance of prayer—especially in the college years.

Some may think prayer means being in a special holy place and addressing God in a deep resonant voice speaking Elizabethan English. Others might think God won't listen to them because they have sinned. The reality is God is perfectly capable of understanding you in whatever tone of voice, using whatever words, in whatever location you happen to be.

Just as you have different kinds of conversations with people, there are different kinds of prayers. No one conversation is better than another. God always listens. The key to talking to God is being totally open and totally honest. Sometimes I find myself needing to talk to God but not knowing what to say. At this point, I ask the Holy Spirit to do the praying—to say the words—for me. Then I listen for His answer as I study His Word.

Prayer and studying God's Word go hand in hand. It's a lifestyle. These two forms of connecting with God give strength and purpose to my life in these confusing years. I discovered that the more time I spent studying God's Word the stronger my prayer life became. In prayer I ask God for direction in reading His Word. I pray to

God to change my life of sin that I might be empowered to live for Him in all I do. I thank God for His faithfulness and blessing in my life. Most of all, I listen.

College convinced me that I was the center of all things. But just as I think I'm on top of things, I find that I'm really not. I really need to listen to God talking to me and telling me what I need to hear. There are still empty times when I really don't feel like praying, or don't feel that I can pray, or don't feel that God listens or even cares. That is when I most need to talk to Him. I tell God how I feel, knowing He won't be shocked—He already knows. Finally I look to the cross and remember Jesus. God abandoned His own Son so Christ could take my sins away. What a blessing that God listens to and answers all my prayer.

> Dear Jesus, help me to connect with You through Your Word and prayer. Help me to block out all the distractions that take me away from You. Help me listen to what You have to say to me. In Your name I pray. Amen.

DEATH OR REAL LIFE?

Read: Psalm 121 and Philippians 1:15–27

Whether you are in college or starting a career it is a time to meet new people. Chances are you have known the same group of friends for possibly four or more years. If you are going away for college or moving away from your home, chances are you are going to meet a whole new group of people. New people, new ideas, new experience—they are all coming your way.

Encountering new people means encountering new or different ideas. You probably know this already. One of the most challenging ideas you may encounter is that life ends at death. Many people believe that life ends then. They don't really know what happens or if anything happens; it's just simply the end. It's not really something they bother to concern themselves with. They just try to squeeze as much fun and pleasure out of life before it's over. But as you get older the death of family members or close friends may cause you to take a closer look at death, although some will still stubbornly refuse.

For Christians death is not something that is scary or to be feared. The Apostle Paul gladly exclaimed that for him "to live is Christ, and to die is gain" (Philippians 1:21). Paul realized that knowing Christ changes your whole mindset on death. It isn't the end of the party, but the start of a new, better, and never-ending one. Heaven is without a doubt a wonderful place that Christ has prepared for us. The extent of the magnificence of heaven will completely overshadow our short little glimpse of time here on earth.

As a result, this changes not only how we face death but also how we look at life here on earth. We don't have to be afraid of dying as if it would be some sort of major tragedy. Without fear we are freed to live our lives for others, especially those without the hope of eternal life. In anticipation of heaven we are aware of the brevity of our time in this world. Whatever time we have (and nowhere are we ever promised a long life) is a gift from God and we use it in service to Him. Paul echoes that sentiment in his letter to the Philippians. Since our time is short, we don't live for ourselves, maximizing our sinful desires. Rather we seek to build each other up spiritually, to point people to Christ. As Paul puts it in Ephesians 5, "live as children of light . . . and find out what pleases the Lord" (verses 8–10). May God grant us grace that we might so live in Him.

> Dear Lord, please keep me ever mindful of the heavenly reward that awaits those found in You. Grant me the opportunities, desire, and courage to serve You. Thank You for sending Your only Son on our behalf so we might have a life that never ends. In His name I pray. Amen.